Economics
Courses

Getting into guides

Getting into

Business & Economics Courses

Justin Edwards

13th edition

Getting into Business & Economics Courses

This 13th edition published in 2019 by Trotman Education, an imprint of Crimson Publishing Ltd, 21d Charles Street, Bath BA1 1HX

© Crimson Publishing Ltd 2019

Author: Justin Edwards
12th edn: Michael McGrath
10th–11th edns: Carly Roberts
8th–9th edns: James Burnett
6th–7th edns: Kate Smith
3rd–5th edns: Fiona Hindle
1st–2nd edns: Trotman, published in 1994 and 1996 as *Getting into Accountancy, Business Studies and Economics*

Editions 1–7 published by Trotman and Co. Ltd

British Library Cataloguing in Publication Data
A catalogue record for this book is available from the British Library

ISBN 978 1 912943 02 9

Printed and bound in Malta by Gutenberg Press Ltd

Contents

Introduction

Congratulations! You've made a very positive first step by deciding that economics and/or business subjects are the direction that you want the next step of your education to take. The choice of subject to study at degree level is often the most difficult choice of all, but this is a subject area that can remain exciting and fresh throughout your career.

This book will provide guidance, information and help with applying for a very broad range of business and economic courses as well as courses related to management, accounting, finance and banking.

One of the appeals of this group of courses is the wealth of career options they can lead on to. In a world where there is an increasing expectation that people will change direction several times during their working lives, keeping doors open and learning transferable skills are particularly important. This family of courses produces graduates that are both literate and numerate and have an interest in the forces that shape their society; graduates are employed in a diverse range of occupations from banking to public policy, from teaching to marketing and journalism. Simply look at the degree choices of senior politicians across the world to note the influence of these graduates on our lives!

About this book

This book is designed to give you an overview of the whole application process as well as to guide you step by step through each stage. It is intended to be read from cover to cover rather than to be dipped into for reference.

Chapter 1 looks at the wide range of options available for students of business and/or economics and related disciplines; it includes a discussion about new degree apprenticeships and the importance of mathematics.

Chapter 2 considers work experience in all its forms, including internships, as well as why work experience is a good idea.

Chapter 3 is about how to choose your university and course. It considers both academic and more personal reasons.

Chapter 4 focuses on the UCAS application and suggests a timescale for completing your application.

Chapter 5 covers the all-important personal statement and how to maximise your chances of your application being successful.

Chapter 6 looks at the university interview, in terms of both preparation and how to behave in the interview itself.

Chapter 7 is for anyone who is not putting forward a standard application to university; mature students as well as international students can find useful information here.

Chapter 8 considers what happens on results day! You may have to reconsider your plans at short notice, including the, perhaps unintentional, gap year; this covers the options that may be available.

Chapter 9 covers fees and the types of funding you may be eligible for.

Chapter 10 discusses some of the career areas that you might think about applying to once you have graduated. This chapter goes into detail about making the first steps in your career and the options open to business and economics graduates.

Chapter 11 brings together useful websites and other resources. It also provides a suggested reading list and thoughts on current issues in business and economics that may help you to find inspiration for your personal statement or as aids to an interview.

Where to start

A good starting point for research is looking at university websites. However, remember these are designed to show the university in a positive light. You can also talk to other people who have been through your experience in the past. Ask them what they would do differently if they had their time again. Always be aware that institutions and courses change over time; parents and teachers may not be the most up-to-date source of information. There are also league tables available, though an important factor to remember is that you are an individual with individual tastes and preferences; what suits others may not suit you. Some useful websites include:

- Times Higher Education: www.timeshighereducation.com/student/ news/national-student-survey-2018-overall-satisfaction-results
- Whatuni: www.whatuni.com/student-awards-winners/university-of-the-year
- Unistats: https://unistats.ac.uk.

Open days are also valuable but beware of taking too much time out of school; your A level results are important so avoid skipping lessons. One student bar or hall of residence looks very much like another. However, researching the people who would be teaching you is recommended. What have they published? What are their areas of interest and expertise? Would that interest you? The course itself and how it is assessed is more important than the choice of beers in the bar.

If you have not studied business or economics at school this is not a problem. It may even prove to be an advantage because your mind will be open, fresh and enquiring when you start your course. However, a degree course is no small undertaking, so you must make sure you know enough about the subject to want to commit to three or four years of study. At the end of this volume, with the list of useful websites, is a recommended reading list.

Work experience will also be an invaluable insight into the subject area. Not only will it help any application, it will also encourage you to consider your career path post university and research what it would actually be like working in a particular field. It will help you decide whether this is really something you want to pursue in practice or whether you just like the idea in theory. Careers in finance may have attractive salaries but the long hours worked may not suit everyone. Work experience and internships are often difficult to get but firms may be more helpful if you ask to spend a day shadowing an employee; especially if the employee is someone you know.

You have the opportunity to make five choices on your UCAS application. Your personal statement will lean towards your first choice, but the application must be suitable for all five choices. Try, if possible, to apply for similar-sounding courses so that you appear focused and committed. A general rule of thumb is to make one or two aspirational choices but to make sure that you also have realistic insurance choices too. The care you take choosing the insurance course is often more important than your dream choice.

Case study

'I hadn't studied economics at school but had a strong maths and politics background. Through my other A level subjects I followed the news and was well informed, and I felt well prepared for my course. On arrival I was surprised by the jump in the way in which I was expected to study. I realised that I had been supported more than I had realised by my teachers at school and that a more independent approach to learning was now required. I would definitely recommend getting into the habit of reading widely during the period leading up to university. Get used to reading newspapers and journals, and follow online blogs as events unfold.'

Sarah, Economics student, London School of Economics

What is economics?

Economics is often described as the 'Dismal Science'; a term used by the writer Thomas Carlyle in the 19th century. It is said that he used this expression because he was disappointed that economists could not find an economic justification for the slave trade. That slavery does not have an economic justification may surprise you, but economics is neither moral or immoral, rather it is a social science.

A scientific approach requires economic theory to stand up to scrutiny and peer review: if different people use the same data in the same way then they ought to reach the same answer. Economic modelling and forecasting is an important, albeit abstract, part of the subject. Econometrics and the link with mathematics and statistics is discussed in Chapter 1, while other branches of economics are considered at the end of this section.

'Thinking like an economist' requires an open mind, a desire for an evidence-based approach to conclusions and a curiosity about the important questions of our time. We are certainly living in interesting times and an economics course will provide you with a 'tool-kit' that gives you valuable, highly sought-after skills that you can apply to most situations; this is perhaps why economics graduates can command high starting salaries in the labour market.

Economists today come in all shapes and sizes as it is a very varied discipline. You may be interested in the following subjects.

- **Economic history.** Some students are surprised by how much history is taught on an economics course, even at A level. For example, many university courses expect first-year students to study the Industrial Revolution.

> **Joke**
>
> Student: 'What was the impact of the French Revolution of 1789 on output and prices?'
>
> Teacher: 'It's far too early to say.'

- **Development economics.** To put it simply; the world has rich countries and poor countries. *Why* this disparity exists is an area for economic analysis, as are the potential solutions that may be required to close these gaps. The first volume to address these issues was Adam Smith's *The Wealth of Nations* (full title: *An Inquiry into the Nature and Causes of the Wealth of Nations*) written in 1776. Karl Marx followed this almost a century later in

1867 with *Das Kapital*, also known as *Capital. Critique of Political Economy*. Many economists work in aid organisations ranging from Oxfam to the World Bank and will have chosen undergraduate courses that focus on development issues.

- **Financial economics.** At A level some aspects of banking and finance are considered; in particular the role of a nation's central bank and sources of business finance, including micro-finance. You could choose a degree course with its focus firmly in these areas. Incidentally, the Bank of England has a fantastic YouTube channel that both educates and entertains.

- **Economic policy.** This looks at the role of governments in setting macroeconomic objectives and also the policy instruments that governments use to attain those objectives. For example, the use of taxation, infrastructure expansion, subsidies, regulation and the other tools that allow the economy to run smoothly and provide a healthy environment for businesses to prosper in.

- **Business economics.** This can be a very theoretical branch of the subject covering the different diagrammatic analyses of different market structures. Knowledge of business economics can add rigour to debates about the role of competition in driving efficiency and the costs of market failure. Business economists may also study game theory and consider the shifts in global trade patterns.

- **Behavioural economics.** This is a relatively modern branch of economics and recognises that standard neoclassical economic theory ignores the psychology of both consumer and business behaviour. If you are interested in how the brain works in decision making – for example, how advertising may influence our behaviour – then this subject area may be worth you exploring.

- **Environmental economics.** Economists are very much at the forefront of debates into the impacts of climate change on global and local economies. They recognise how the weaknesses in neoclassical analysis may have contributed to these problems and are actively looking for mechanisms to harness economic incentives to find solutions. Economists can comment with authority on issues ranging from plastic pollution in oceans to desertification in the Sahel region of Africa and flood risks in the River Ganges catchment in India. It is economists who are encouraging the shift from fossil fuels to solar energy through the free market mechanism and who understand how carbon taxes may work.

The above is not an exhaustive list. The length of the list may go some way to explain economists' perhaps favourite Winston Churchill quote: 'If you put two economists in a room, you get two opinions, unless one of them is Lord Keynes, in which case you get three opinions.'

What about business studies?

In some ways business studies is more straightforward to explain than economics: it could be described as narrower yet deeper. While many schools do offer Business Studies A level, as a 'non-preferred' subject some of you may have been discouraged from choosing it. Although a business degree does not necessarily qualify you for a specific career path – see professional accreditation on page 17 – it may give you insight into the causes of business failure and help you if you aspire to start your own business in the future. However, if you already know that you want to train as an accountant, then you may be wise to look at apprenticeships rather than degree courses (see Chapter 1).

Business studies degrees vary considerably because they are offered by so many institutions, from the most highly ranked to the more modest. The most highly ranked courses will expect more from you and may offer professional accreditation, but at the lower-ranked institutions you may find a more supportive teaching staff with practical experience of specific businesses.

Typically, a business-related course will cover some, if not all, of the following.

- **Marketing.** This is a very broad area covering everything from pricing strategies to budgets for promotional activities. At A level, business students will learn about the 'Marketing Mix' – the four Ps of Price, Place, Promotion and Product. Marketing courses look at market research and you may be expected to use statistical analysis to identify trends and to assess the significance of your findings. Product development is a related subject but may require more practical skills in particular fields, such as engineering or the creative arts, for example.

- **Business and commercial law.** Business operations face a wide range of regulation, much of it statutory. Regulation will cover employment, financial reporting, local planning and licencing plus waste disposal and pollution control. Businesses may also trade across international borders and knowledge of the relevant law can be very useful. There are many Business Law Joint Honours degrees available.

- **Finance and Accounts.** This, too, is a broad area, with both specialist and more general approaches. You may look at the day-to-day finances of a business and budgeting, or at long-term financial planning and investments including sources of finance and financial reporting. A simple way of understanding the difference between the two is; finance looks *ahead* to what *will* happen, and accounting looks *back* at what *has* happened. Don't worry if you're not very confident in mathematics; accountants deal with numbers that represent something real rather than the more abstract concepts that mathematicians love.

- **Operations management.** This is concerned with efficiency within a business, in particular productive efficiency. A profitable business is not wasteful, and this area looks at different systems, often in manufacturing, that help limit wastefulness. Japanese systems, such as 'just-in-time' (JIT) and 'continuous improvement', are relevant here as are 'critical path analysis' (CPA) and 'decision trees'.

- **Human resource management.** Business magnate Bill Gates once said: 'The inventory, the value of your company, walks out the door every evening.' Businesses know that if they want happy customers then the business staff has to be happy too. Management of people is certainly not easy and the issues surrounding human capital will form a central part of a degree course in business. There are fashions and trends regarding the psychology of management as well as many different theories of motivation that you will study. Some of the most prestigious courses at British universities have the word 'management' in their degree title as a reflection of the importance of this topic area.

- **Macroeconomics.** All business courses will include elements of economics, and whereas micro topics such as the 'price elasticity of demand' will be covered in marketing, the wider business environment also requires study. Businesses do not operate in a vacuum; so issues such as unemployment, inflation, interest rates, business and consumer confidence, external shocks and economic growth rates are taught. You may also look at issues such as immigration, terrorism, refugees, homelessness and nationalism as these topics inevitably impact on businesses.

- **Communication.** Some of the greatest recent changes that businesses have witnessed fall into this category; whether it's the rise of internet shopping, contactless payments or consumer campaigns orchestrated through social media. The IT (information technology) department is an important component of all businesses in the modern era.

- **International trade.** Entrepreneurial businesses have always traded across international boundaries; for example, Vikings from Scandinavia traded with the Far East through the important hub that was Constantinople (modern Istanbul in Turkey), even leaving Viking graffiti in the Hagia Sophia there. Trade theory and regulation is part of most business courses, as is looking quite closely at how governments support businesses who wish to trade overseas. Many students who are interested in the international aspects of business also choose to study a language as part of their degree.

Your degree is a big investment that may lead to a debt that takes some years to repay, so make sure that you have considered the return that you expect on that investment. It also perhaps goes without saying that to get the most out of your investment you must work hard and take advantage of all the opportunities that your chosen university can offer to enhance your CV and help you in competitive labour markets in the future.

1 | Studying business, economics and related courses

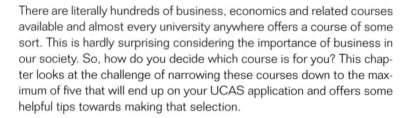

There are literally hundreds of business, economics and related courses available and almost every university anywhere offers a course of some sort. This is hardly surprising considering the importance of business in our society. So, how do you decide which course is for you? This chapter looks at the challenge of narrowing these courses down to the maximum of five that will end up on your UCAS application and offers some helpful tips towards making that selection.

Course titles

Today, almost all universities employ marketing teams to make their prospectuses sound exciting and attractive. They give courses creative and exciting titles too, but remember that despite the attractive packaging the course content can often be fairly similar across the board. Some of the potential courses you could take include:

- accounting and finance
- banking and finance
- business and management studies
- business, mathematics and statistics
- business studies
- econometrics and mathematical economics
- economics
- financial economics
- management (three-year course)
- management (four-year sandwich course)
- management sciences
- mathematics and economics.

Most universities have core subject content that they teach across the faculty, regardless of which degree course you are enrolled on. This means that in your first year you can expect to be taught in large lecture theatres with maybe hundreds of other students. The details of core subject content can be found in the prospectus. Often you don't start to specialise in your chosen field until the second or even third year. This may give you the opportunity to switch on to a slightly different course at a later date if you find that your interests have shifted. However, do *not* gamble on this possibility, as different universities have different policies – so it is best to make the best choice for you from the start.

Single or joint honours?

Joint honours programmes, such as economics and business management, may be a good option for those who are unsure about what career they would like to pursue after graduation. While these degrees can be very rewarding, you should look closely at the small print as some joint degrees offer diluted versions of both subjects whereas others double the workload. Or, some may not be true joint degrees but more of a conglomerate, such as economics *with* business management; yet these courses too may offer the more wide-ranging course content that some students are looking for.

It is recommended to consider courses that may offer extra support in helping you get your dream job in the future. For example, if you want to work in an international setting and travel a lot then maybe consider keeping a language option open. Or, if you want to work in overseas aid then maybe investigate studying geography or development studies alongside economics or management. Of course, one of the most prestigious and competitive courses in this general area is PPE – Politics, Philosophy and Economics. This whole area is well worth discussing with your friends, family and teachers just to gather a range of opinions. But at the end of the day you must make your own decision.

TIP!

Read the course title and content breakdowns carefully. Make sure you know what the differences are between the different options available.

Case study

'When I tell people that I graduated with a joint honours degree I'm often greeted with some baffled responses because they are two completely different subjects; people don't see the connection between the two, and, consequently, think that the lack of clear connection is a bad thing. But after explaining how many different opportunities doing two quite different courses gave me, and that I now have the option to move into a broad and varied range of jobs, people are quick to change their opinion. Graduating with joint honours simply means that I have one degree in two subjects. Employers don't see a joint honours degree in a negative way, thinking it's only 50% each of two subjects. Rather, having a degree in two subjects can increase your chances of finding work when you graduate. For example, it can be beneficial for those who want to teach because you can show potential employers that you have expertise in two subjects and so can apply to teach in two different areas.

'When choosing a single honours course, the classes that you can choose are often more fixed and chosen for you. Choosing a joint honours degree can allow you to select the modules that you want to do, giving you more flexibility. Therefore, if there are certain classes you won't enjoy, or won't be very good at, you can (providing they are not mandatory and your timetable allows you to do so) miss those out and pick other ones that suit you.'

Alex, University of Worcester

How much mathematics do I want to study?

This is a tricky conundrum. You must expect to develop numeracy skills on any business and economics course. You are unlikely to be able to avoid calculating price elasticities and using/interpreting statistical data wherever or whatever you choose to study in this subject area. Accountancy courses will obviously expect some number crunching, but managers and marketing teams also use numbers. Economists use high-level mathematics in forecasting and modelling, and then there is econometrics.

Econometrics is very much about using statistics and methods such as 'regression' to make models to explain economic activity. To quote Paul Samuelson et al in 1954 '*[econometrics is] the quantitative analysis of actual economic* **phenomena** *based on the concurrent development of theory and observation, related by appropriate methods of inference.*' In other words, econometricians enjoy solving puzzles and problems using mathematical tools.

In recent years some economics, business and finance courses have started to include mention of 'quantitative methods' as a study option. Quantitative research is rigorous when it comes to data collection, so that the methods used to display, explain and analyse the findings stand up to close scrutiny and research results can be duplicated, thus making conclusions more convincing. These courses are unlikely to suit you if you feel faint at the sight of a row of figures.

On the other hand, some economics departments are starting to move away from an emphasis on mathematical proofs in recognition that, if the data used is unconvincing, then however convincing and complicated the mathematical analysis is, the theory is built on a weak foundation. You may be already aware of the student movement at the University of Manchester that pushed towards learning more 'real' economics. If you are interested in these alternative views, a useful place to start finding out more may be the website of the pressure group Rethinking Economics, www.rethinkeconomics.org/about/our-story.

Case study

'My degree had a strong focus on econometrics, although there was a wide range of optional units to choose from, and I enjoyed the opportunity I had to study in the Far East in my final year. Most of the teaching was conducted in large lecture theatres, making it sometimes difficult to pick up the abstract concepts quickly; there was equation after equation after equation! Almost every unit was assessed by a single three-hour exam at the end, and in my whole time at university I only submitted two essays and my dissertation for marking. This suited me but I know that some of my friends struggled.'

Grace, economics graduate

Methods of assessment and approaches to learning

As an A level (or equivalent) student you ought to have a good idea by now about how you like to learn and how you prefer to be assessed. Different universities approach teaching in different ways and offer differing amounts of contact time with tutors and lecturers. Often universities that are renowned for research offer courses that offer the least contact time while the lower ranking institutions may offer far more student support. If you are disciplined and enjoy private study then the amount of contact with staff may matter less to you than it would to someone with less confidence in their ability to study with minimal supervision. Likewise, some students enjoy the pressure of high-stake examinations while others prefer more continuous assessment and alternatives to traditional examinations. And some universities, but not all, make a dissertation a compulsory course unit. A close study of the various prospectuses will help you to choose a course that suits you.

If you have additional or special educational needs and have received extra time in examinations in the past, then your university will continue to support you with this, so long as you tell them in good time. They may re-test you because the rules regarding extra time change every so often. You may be interested to know that in Norway examinations are rarely time-limited so that all students have an opportunity to shine.

> **TIP!**
>
> Check if the course matches your strengths and weaknesses. Investigate methods and frequency of assessment.

How many years should I study for?

When tuition fees were first introduced it was hoped that by introducing elements of a free market to higher education then different universities would compete for students by offering different fee structures as well as different courses. This did not come to pass and most universities charge the maximum fee allowed.

Sandwich courses

Business and economics courses often have the option of a year in industry and/or abroad on a placement. These types of courses are sometimes called sandwich courses. These can be very attractive options to students looking to broaden their horizons and to gain skills that will help them to stand out in competitive job markets in the future. Consequently, these are four-year courses rather than the standard three. There may be tuition fees charged for this placement year so please check the small print. The support offered finding placements also varies from place to place, and some students struggle to find appropriate placements, particularly when there is a lack of confidence in the wider business community.

> **TIP!**
>
> Think very hard about the financial implications to you and your family when considering a four-year course.

Two-year courses

There are now also a handful of universities offering intensive two-year courses – and some with a January start rather than the traditional October. These are designed for more mature students returning to education to enhance their skills, but could also be attractive to students concerned about the levels of personal debt that they may accumulate during a three- or four-year course. If you have ever wondered why university students have such long breaks between terms, and if the potential to waste time frustrates you, then you may wish to look at these two-year courses. If there proves to be a significant demand for shorter courses, then more universities may well start to offer them. At the end of 2018 the UK government announced that it was going to encourage universities to offer shorter courses.

Foundation years and Foundation degrees

These should not be confused!

Foundation year

A Foundation year is designed for students who do not meet the formal entry requirements for a standard three-year course. This could be because they are more mature students who have been out of education for a while and did not previously believe that they were interested in further education; or those with non-standard school qualifications, such as some overseas qualifications; or those whose personal circumstances disrupted their studies at school. If you 'pass' your Foundation year you can then embark on a three-year course. Consequently you will complete your degree over four years with the related extra tuition and living costs to consider.

Foundation degree

A Foundation degree is considered to be the equivalent of two-thirds of a standard bachelor's degree and often involves learning workplace skills as well as academic study. These were introduced in 2001 in order to help improve the nation's skills. Many people with Foundation degrees carry on and 'top up' by completing a fourth year – not necessarily at the same institution or immediately after – but topping up may not be required depending on your career aspirations. Some graduate schemes do consider applicants with Foundation degrees because they take into account critical thinking skills, work experience and other life skills, as well as academic qualifications; some of the big accountancy firms fall into this category. The current chronic labour shortage in some key sectors makes Foundation degrees an increasingly attractive option for those who find the prospect of an intensive academic course daunting.

Overseas study

Many students these days are attracted by the thought of completing their studies overseas rather than in the UK. Overseas universities feature prominently in the global university league tables. There is a lot to be said in favour of these options, particularly for economics and business students, because of the global nature of markets and businesses in the modern world. English is said to be the language of international business, so many courses, even in countries such as Italy or Germany, are taught in English. The cost of studying for a degree in Germany for a British national can be significantly cheaper than studying in the UK; whereas studying in the USA or Australia can be considerably more expensive.

If you choose to study abroad and have English as a first language, you may be able to find casual work locally in bars and hotels because of your spoken English. In turn, you may have the opportunity to pick up the local language. Of course, the great unknown is the changes there may be to the UK's relationship with the rest of the European Union in the future. We probably won't know for several years exactly what a European degree may mean in UK labour markets, and for now the safer option may be to choose a degree course at a British university that offers the opportunity of overseas study as part of their programme. Needless to say, if you are interested in this route a lot of careful research is required.

The UCAS website (www.ucas.com) offers some support in helping you to make a start, as does www.prospects.ac.uk.

Higher apprenticeships and degree apprenticeships

You may decide that a standard university degree does not offer value for money, particularly if it may still lead to you having to study for vocational qualifications afterwards. This is particularly true if you are considering a future career in one of the many branches of accountancy.

An exciting recent change in further education has been the introduction, and rapid expansion of, degree-equivalent apprenticeships. These can involve joining an employer on completion of A levels and your employer will train you and maybe guide you through professional qualifications. Some of these schemes work in partnership with a university or college and at the end of the apprenticeship you will have a degree or credits towards a degree. According to the UCAS website, in 2018 over 70 universities, and around 200 colleges, were approved to deliver higher and degree apprenticeships.

Higher apprenticeships

Higher apprenticeship refers to all apprenticeships that include the achievement of academic/vocational qualifications from level 4 (in higher eduation qualifications, an A level is equivalent to a level 3 qualification) up to bachelor's and master's degree at level 6–7.

Degree Apprenticeships

Degree apprenticeships see apprentices achieving a full bachelor's or master's degree (levels 6 and 7) as a core component of the apprenticeship.

Pros

1. You 'learn while you earn'. This means that you will not potentially be accumulating debt while you study but rather will have the freedom associated with having an independent income.

2. You will be three years ahead of those who join the same firm as graduates. You will have had the opportunity to impress your employers, and often the school-leaver schemes are less competitive than the graduate entry schemes.

Cons

1. You may feel that you are channelling yourself into a particular career path before you are fully aware of all the opportunities available.

2. You will miss out on the cultural rite of passage that is university, with the opportunity it offers to broaden your horizons and meet a huge range of different people from different backgrounds.

3. Neither apprenticeship is eligible for a student loan.

There are a myriad of different opportunities and they change from year to year, so you will need to be proactive – treat it as you would if you were looking for employment opportunities. All the leading accountancy firms, banks and consultants offer their own variations of the schemes.

Many school teachers and parents are unaware of these new opportunities and there is an expectation that academically able and ambitious students will go to university in the traditional manner. Many schools do offer access to professional career advice services and these may be able to furnish you with more information than your teachers have available to them. The UCAS website is also very helpful, as is the UK Government National Apprenticeship Service (www.gov.uk/apply-apprenticeship).

> ## Case study: Degree vs apprenticeship
>
> ### Degree
>
> Frank chose the traditional route. He went to a Russell Group university and studied 'straight' economics. He was hard-working and conscientious and graduated with a first class degree. In his final year he had applied for graduate schemes and taken advantage of contacts he made during the National Citizenship Service scheme and through a Social Mobility Foundation internship scheme; both schemes he had followed while at school. He now has a graduate placement with an international bank in London; he will continue to study for his professional qualifications.
>
> ### Apprenticeship
>
> At school Adam was less sure than Frank of where he wanted life to take him; he was also nervous of student debt. Adam applied for, and was accepted on, several apprenticeship schemes. After a lot of procrastination he chose to join a Civil Service scheme in Whitehall. After only 12 months his mentors recommended that he apply for the prestigious Civil Service Fast Stream graduate leadership development programme. He duly did so, competing for scarce places with graduates from top universities. The extra confidence that resulted from his understanding of the workplace enabled him to shine at the selection events. Now, at 21, he has a position in the Home Office and is working towards his professional accountancy qualifications.

Professional accreditation

It is very likely that you will have to do some professional training as a business and/or economics graduate. For example, you may be considering a career in accountancy, and in this case your employer will support you with the training and study leave so that you can complete your professional qualification. The same will also apply to some other careers in business, banking and management.

Your degree course may give you some exemptions in the form of 'credits' towards these qualifications so that you can qualify more quickly than graduates from other disciplines. The individual university prospectuses will guide you regarding this, as will the professional bodies themselves. For example, the Institute of Chartered Accountants website (https://careers.icaew.com) mentions a degree course at the University of Liverpool that covers all 12 modules that you need to complete to qualify as a chartered accountant. Another useful website is   Bright   Network   (www.brightnetwork.co.uk/career-path-guides/accounting-audit-tax/how-to-job-accounting-financial-management/guide-to-accounting-qualifications).

2 | Getting work experience

The top universities, i.e. those that 'select' rather than 'recruit', look for applications that stand out from the crowd. There are plenty of students with A-grade predictions and play for the sports A team, but there are not as many who can demonstrate how committed they are to their chosen subject by having completed relevant work experience or undertaken some other preparation for employment scheme. It is therefore well worth looking for work experience while you are studying for your A levels.

Admissions tutors want to see evidence that you're a good time manager, too. They do not want students who miss lectures because they can't get out of bed in the morning, so evidence that you can hold down a job is also useful. The beauty of studying a business-related course at university is that all your holiday jobs and Saturday jobs – even a humble paper round – can give you valuable experience of the wider business environment, and therefore used to show your commitment to a business-related course.

As you may well end up working until you're 70 years old, a gap year between school and university may seem an attractive option right now. This is certainly worth considering *if* it helps you gain experience of the real world of work. You may not have found time while at school to hold a part-time job, so a spell in the labour force would enhance your university application as well as helping you to gain skills that will certainly appeal to prospective employers on graduation. Remember, however, that a gap year solely involving beaches in South-East Asia will not count as relevant work experience, even if it proves that you can live away from home.

Most university economics and business departments encourage their students to gain work experience and attend networking events during their three or four years of study. This is, in part, why courses in cities that are home to many firms in the financial sector are often more attractive to students and hence more competitive when it comes to securing a place.

This chapter will focus on what you can do *prior* to university to enhance your future prospects at the institution of your choice.

> 'Your extra-curricular activities such as work experience ... are important, particularly when they can provide evidence of useful skills such as problem solving, working under pressure and time management ...'
>
> London School of Economics
>
> 'All the candidates' interests outside their academic studies assist selection by providing valuable background information.'
>
> Imperial College, London
>
> 'We need to see evidence that your interest is genuine: If a degree is related to a particular line of work, that you have work experience ... or can demonstrate you understand what the profession involves.'
>
> University of Birmingham

What is work experience?

Work experience covers everything from actual employment through work placements and internships to shadowing, networking events and volunteering. All of these are valuable and can be presented in such a way as to highlight the knowledge and skills you have gained. There has been a lot of media coverage over the years about the inequity surrounding internships, particularly unpaid work placements, and therefore a placement in a very prestigious organisation may say more about your socio-economic background than it does about your commitment to a particular career path. The experience you gain through your own efforts is what the admissions tutors are looking for.

Where to find work experience

Unfortunately, opportunities are becoming increasingly scarce. When offering work experience, businesses have to consider everything from commercial confidentiality to health and safety. They also need to be able to offer meaningful experience (although releasing a paper jam from the photocopier could be considered a valuable skill!). Therefore, if there is a particular business you want to approach, ask if you could *shadow* an employee in a particular role for a day or so. This may relieve the company's concerns about how to accommodate you and make them more willing to be helpful. They may then even allow you to follow up by shadowing other employees in other roles, and hence you may gain valuable insight into several possible future careers.

Start by talking to your teachers, friends, family and anyone who will listen! Teachers may have contacts and most schools have an alumnus network where former students offer to help current students. LinkedIn can prove a valuable resource, too.

Your school library or school notice board may hold careers information. Local firms may have out-reach programmes where they want to make connections with your school as part of showing their commitment to social responsibility in the local area, and the librarian or Head of Sixth Form may be holding this information.

There are also some excellent schemes on offer that are very prestigious and have very competitive application processes that your school may be able to help you with. One such scheme is the Social Mobility Foundation's Aspiring Professionals Scheme (www.socialmobility.org. uk). This is particularly designed for young people from socially deprived backgrounds. Alternatively, the National Citizenship Programme (www. ncsyes.co.uk/what-is-ncs) is a scheme to help young people become engaged in their local communities, and does not limit who can apply to participate. In both of these schemes businesses act as mentors so they can become useful points of contact for help in the future.

If you already have part-time work, maybe in retail, you could do worse than ask to spend some time in their accounts or marketing departments. Volunteer to take extra responsibility, such as helping at closing time, and talk to the managers about their work. Don't be the casual worker who is the last to arrive and the first to leave – your employer may be asked to provide a valuable reference for you one day. If you don't have a weekend or holiday job, then this is something you should consider too. Although ensure that it does not conflict with the time you need for academic study.

Many schools offer an annual programme called Young Enterprise. This is something students usually sign up to in Year 12 and is not exclusively for business studies students. The scheme involves developing entrepreneurial skills in conjunction with an advisor from the local business community. These advisors will also be very helpful when you are looking for work experience and the scheme also offers great opportunities for networking. Even if you have left it too late to join Young Enterprise, it is worth speaking to the teacher in charge and ask to be introduced to the advisors.

There are many other similar schemes to those detailed above.

There is no single guaranteed way of getting work experience, so try as many ways as you can think of, and be creative in the process. Here are a few suggestions.

- Ask your teachers at school/college if they have any contacts in the business world.

- Use your careers library and speak to your careers officer.
- Talk to your family and friends and ask them whether they can suggest anyone to contact.
- Make sure everyone you know is aware you are looking for work experience.
- Send your CV and a covering letter to a variety of local businesses.
- Keep up to date by reading the business pages of broadsheets and watching and listening to business programmes on television and radio.
- Look around at volunteering websites for opportunities relevant to your area of interest.

Volunteering

Voluntary work is another way of gaining work experience and ought not to be confused with unpaid internships. Volunteering will help your application to stand out. Although programmes completed within the school environment, such as Duke of Edinburgh or World Challenge, are less impressive than an experience that you have sought out and organised yourself, they are still worthwhile. You may struggle to find an opening in a volunteering organisation that directly relates to business and economics, but you will certainly gain a range of transferable skills.

Websites and organisations that can help you find an opening.

- TimeBank: https://timebank.org.uk
- Do-it Trust: https://do-it.org
- Youth Action: www.youthaction.org.uk
- vinspired: https://vinspired.com
- Volunteering Matters: https://volunteeringmatters.org.uk

You may also find opportunities through local places of worship, sports teams and the Girl Guides or Scouts. A word of warning, however, some of the volunteering organisations you may find online will expect you to pay or to make a 'donation' in exchange for the opportunity to work with them.

How to put together a CV to apply for work experience

It is never too early to start to put together a CV – a summary of what you have done in your life to date. If you have hardly any work experience, then one page on good-quality A4 paper will be sufficient. If you are a mature student with a lot of jobs behind you, there is sometimes a case for going on to a second page. Always highlight your good points on a CV. And always account for your time – do not leave gaps. If something such as illness prevented you from reaching your potential in your exams, point this out in your covering letter. To succeed in business you need to have excellent attention to detail, so make sure your spelling and grammar are perfect! Lay out your CV clearly and logically. The main headings to cover are described below, and an example CV can be seen on page 24.

Name and contact details

These are the basic details to head your CV. Make sure they're right!

Education and qualifications

Start with your present course of study and work back to the beginning of secondary school. List the qualifications and grades you already have and those you intend to sit.

Work experience

Start with the most recent. Don't worry if you have had only a Saturday job at the local shop or a paper round; put it all down. Employers would rather see that you have done something, and any job will teach you skills, such as reliability or retail skills.

Skills

List everything you do that could have a commercial application, such as computer skills, software packages used, typing, languages, driving licence and so on.

Interests and positions of responsibility

What do you like to do in your spare time? If you hold or have held any positions of responsibility, such as captain of a sports team, a committee member or school prefect, put it all down. Do you play an instrument or have a creative hobby? Do you belong to a society or club? All these say something about the person you are.

Referees

You should provide two referees: an academic one, such as a teacher or the head of your school, plus someone who knows you well personally but is not a relative, such as someone you have worked for.

A sample CV

Mary Coleman

Address 1 Kinrose Lane, Derby DE6 7HP
Telephone 0123 456 7890
Email lmj@melchester.sch.uk

Education 2011–2018: Derby Academy
2018: A levels to be taken: French, Mathematics, Politics
2016: GCSEs: English (A), Mathematics (A), Geography (A),
German (A), Biology (B), Chemistry (B), History (C), Physics (C)

Work experience
August 2016 – present (weekends and some evenings)

Assistant sales manager in Derby County FC official merchandise
store at Pride Park Stadium, Derby.

July 2015

Three weeks as temporary receptionist in plastic moulding
company, responsible for answering telephone and general
clerical work.

2013–2015 (Saturdays)

Delivering newspapers and magazines throughout my local area.

Skills
Modern languages: good written and spoken French.
Good practical mathematics from working at Pride Park Stadium.
IT: competent in MS Word and Excel, good keyboard skills.

Positions of responsibility
Responsible for three staff at Pride Park Stadium.
School Council member in Year 10 and Year 11.
Treasurer for Young Enterprise company.

Interests
Reading, travel, music and Derby County FC.

References
Available on request.

The covering letter

Every CV or application form should always be accompanied by a
covering letter. The letter is important because it is usually the first thing
a potential employer reads. Here are some tips on structuring and pre-
senting your letter.

- The letter should be on the same plain A4 paper as your CV and should look like a professional business document – do not use lined paper. Keep it to a single page only.
- Try to find out the name of the person to whom you should send your letter and CV. It makes a great difference to the reader if you can personalise your application – but do not be overly familiar. Use their title (Mr, Ms, Dr, etc.) and last name, not 'Dear Bob'. Refer to a book or webpage on business letter writing if you need help with the conventions. For example, if you start the letter 'Dear Mr Brown' remember you should finish it 'Yours sincerely'. If you do not know the recipient's name and send it, for example, to the personnel manager, begin with 'Dear Sir or Madam' and finish with 'Yours faithfully'.
- The first paragraph should tell the reader why you are contacting them. For example, 'I am writing to enquire whether you have any openings for work experience.'.
- The second paragraph should attempt to engage them by highlighting your interest in business, along with some specific skills you can offer, such as knowledge of word processing or having a good telephone manner.
- Say in the letter whether you know anything about the company and how you found out about it (for example, if friends or family work there) or whether you've read anything recently that was of interest or was relevant to your career prospects.
- Employers usually prefer typed letters, unless they specifically request one to be handwritten.

Whether you are applying for a position through an advertisement or just sending a speculative letter to a local company, you should do plenty of research on the employer. Having some information will help you tailor your CV for that particular company, and it will certainly be impressive if, at interview, you show some knowledge of how the company works.

If you have an application form to fill in, follow the instructions carefully. Always complete forms neatly, using black ink. If your handwriting can be unclear, make sure that you take your time. With application forms, you probably will not be asked to submit your CV as well, so always include evidence about your skills and interests in the statements in the form. Most of these forms are online, so if you make a mistake, print another copy and start again. A sloppy application will not be helpful, even if the content makes you a strong candidate.

It is imperative that you keep copies of all the letters, CVs and application forms you send off, not just so you can remember to whom you have applied but so you have something to work from at an interview. You are bound to be asked to elaborate on things you have written about yourself, so do not say you have a skill or an interest if you cannot back it up.

Work experience interviews

Most of the tips from Chapter 6 – Succeeding at interview are equally useful if you are going for a work experience interview. However, here are some additional pointers.

- Think through why you want the job, and in particular why you want to work for that organisation.
- Research the employer thoroughly before the interview. Look at their brochure and website.
- Plan in advance what you think your key selling points are for the employer and make sure you find an opportunity in the interview to get these across.
- Think up a few relevant questions to ask your interviewer at the end. You can demonstrate your preparation here by asking them about something you have read about the company recently, if appropriate.

You should dress smartly, but not too formal. Look at the person speaking and answer in clear and simple language. Follow your parents' advice to sit up straight in your chair. Humour is best avoided. Remember to offer a nice, firm, confident handshake at both the beginning and end of the interview. Be confident without lapsing into arrogance.

Making the most of your work experience

You've gone through all of the above steps to secure yourself a work experience placement, but simply having spent some time in a business is not enough. You need to make sure you can demonstrate exactly what you have got from the experience. The very best work experience will hopefully bring you into contact with people who will help you in the future. Perhaps by simply casting an eye over your personal statement, by offering to write a reference or by being someone you can turn to for advice about employment opportunities or office etiquette. At the very least, your work placement will provide you with experiences – both good and bad – that you can learn from and use to enhance your personal statement and future job applications.

Here are some tips for making your experience really count.

1. **Keep a diary.** Keep detailed notes as a record of everything you do. Record everything that you witness and are working on. Learn the technical vocabulary and ask questions at appropriate times if you need clarification about the purpose of an activity or the meaning of an acronym. Your diary will help you to remember what you did and, more importantly, what you learned from your experiences. You'll be able to draw on it when writing your personal statement and going to any interviews. Saying you have picked up new skills is almost

useless without evidence, so writing things down will mean you can back up your claims later.

2. **Impress.** It isn't enough to just be there: make sure you are on time, presentable and enthusiastic. The employer will want to know that you value the experience, so show them that you are taking it seriously. While you are working, be aware that you will not be conscious of the status of everyone who may see you; so aim to always be the best version of yourself.

3. **Be seen to be enthusiastic and professional.** Those around you are likely to be busy, so you may need to get yourself noticed (in a good way!). If you have finished something, make sure you ask for something else to do, and ask questions to show that you are interested in what you are doing.

4. **Behave appropriately.** Being friendly is essential, but make sure you keep it professional. You are not there to make friends but to get valuable experience, so don't get drawn into office politics and remember you could need to call on any of your colleagues for help or as a reference at some point in the future. Be helpful and polite. Leave your mobile phone switched off and in your bag.

5. **Be organised.** If you do all your work excellently but leave a trail of scrap paper everywhere you will be remembered for the wrong reasons.

6. **Network.** We're not talking about adding your new boss on Facebook (see number 4 – behave appropriately!); this is about making a good impression so that you can come back to people if it might be useful later on. You'll be surprised how often you'll need to call on the help of others for references or advice, and those who get ahead seem to have networking down to a fine art. Before you leave, ask key staff if you could take their email addresses and if they would mind you contacting them if you need advice. If you think it would be useful to get more experience at the company or an in-

---

Case study

Jinaid secured a week-long placement with one of the big four accounting firms. This was unpaid but they did pay his commuting costs and provide him with lunch. At the end of the week he was asked to give a presentation to a group of senior staff about how he would attract new clients to the firm. He understandably found this very daunting, but the experience gave his confidence an enormous boost. The firm was so impressed that it contacted his school 12 months later to offer a placement to another student.

ternship (see below), ask your employer if there might be any opportunities coming up.

7. **Follow up.** Be thankful for the opportunities offered and make sure that you write to thank everyone involved for the experience when you finish. If all goes well you may be invited back for further experience or paid work in the future.

What will you gain from work experience?

- It will add weight to your personal statement.
- It will give you a true insight into the business or financial world and whether or not it is what you want to do. Some real experience will be particularly useful if you are trying to weigh up which area of business you'd like to go into. For example, are you more analytical or creative? Would you be more suited to a career in finance or marketing?
- It will eventually help with the transition from education into the world of full-time work.
- It will give you the opportunity to build up those all-important contacts through networking.
- It will enhance your curriculum vitae (CV) and may help you to gain excellent references.

Internships

Internships are often undertaken while you are at university. Some employers see summer internship programmes as an extended interview process, with top interns being offered jobs when they graduate. With this in mind, you should be checking what sort of support is available at the universities you are considering. Will they help you find a placement? What are the graduate employment figures like? Is there an opportunity to do a year in industry?

Internships come in all shapes and sizes. Some are over the summer holidays, while some are part-time alongside your studies, particularly after the second year of a course. It's never too early to start making links, as finding a work placement can often be half the battle. Opening up useful contacts by doing volunteering and work experience before university could prove very beneficial.

3 | Choosing your university

You have read Chapter 1 and you are starting to develop a clearer picture of the types of business-related courses available. You are minded to go to university in the UK and study for a degree, and are aware of the differences between single and joint honours degrees. You have also thought about the length of course and the type of course content you would prefer. Now you need to think of *where* in the UK to apply to.

England

The Office for Students (OfS, www.officeforstudents.org.uk) takes care of the interests of students in England and is responsible for deciding which institutions have degree-awarding powers and also which institutions can call themselves universities. The OfS started work in January 2018 and brought together the Higher Education Funding Council for England and the Office for Fair Access; it falls under the remit of the Department for Education and there is a Minister of State responsible for Higher Education. It also administers the Teaching Excellence Framework, which monitors the quality of teaching at universities in England.

Wales

Universities in Wales are regulated and funded by the Welsh government.

Scotland

Universities in Scotland are regulated and funded by the Scottish government.

Northern Ireland

Northern Ireland has no higher education funding council; degree courses are administered by the Department for the Economy.

The choice of where – and how – you apply to university is a complex one and there are many factors you will need to take into account. However, as most of you will be applying in the traditional manner through

UCAS the focus of this chapter will be on making those all-important *five* choices.

Competition for places

Entrance requirements for business- and economics-related courses at universities vary enormously. As a general point though, prior subject knowledge is not usually a requirement, even for 'straight' economics degrees. This is partly a recognition that economics is very difficult to staff and so you're lucky if you attend a school that offers it.

It can be useful to make a distinction between universities that *select* their students and universities that *recruit* their students.

'Recruiting' universities

Universities that 'recruit' are competing for your business rather than the other way around; you are considered a valuable asset. As you are paying a not insignificant sum to study for your degree, you have the power in the market, so make sure that you get a deal that suits you. If you have studied either business studies or economics at A level then you know that the consumer has power, is sovereign; that demand leads supply and that the customer is always right. In recent years many universities have started making unconditional offers to the students that they want – a sure sign of your importance to them.

'Selecting' universities

Universities that 'select' their students are those where competition for places is often intense. For these universities a weak application can spoil your chance of being made an offer.

The selective universities include the 24 institutions that make up the Russell Group, which has a list of what they call 'facilitating' A level subjects – subjects that will enhance the prospect of you being offered a place. The current list is:

- mathematics and further mathematics
- English literature
- physics
- biology
- chemistry
- geography
- history
- languages (classical and modern).

The Russell Group states that there is little chance of your application being successful if you cannot offer at least one of these subjects. The Russell Group also publishes a helpful guide called *Informed Choices*, which is available to download from https://russellgroup.ac.uk.

Past and predicted academic performance

Whether you like it or not, the success of your application will depend, to a large extent, on your predicted A level (or equivalent) grades and any past examination results, as this is what selection will be largely based on. If you don't meet the requirements your application will be rejected automatically by the computer or by secretarial staff before it even reaches an admissions officer. If you have any anxieties contact the admissions department directly before you submit your application. This may save a lot of heartache later.

In general the requirements for economics courses are often – but not always – higher than for business courses. For both, however, your mathematics ability is critical. Even if your chosen universities do not insist on A level they may ask for a grade B/5 or 6 at GCSE or equivalent. However, many institutions *do* expect Mathematics A level and sometimes Further Mathematics as well for competitive economics courses, even if the prospectus doesn't say so. It is worth asking admissions officers directly if you are concerned.

> **TIP!**
>
> Check the entry requirements carefully in the prospectuses and on the university departments' websites.

> 'Before you apply, look at the university requirements. Due to the mathematics and statistics included in an economics degree, many universities specify a certain minimum grade at GCSE Mathematics and some require A level Mathematics. At a small number of institutions, further mathematics may be desirable. A level Economics is not essential; studying both economics and business studies at A level should, as a rule, be avoided. In some cases, candidates offering three A levels that include further mathematics may be disadvantaged, as this will be expected as a fourth A level and may not count towards offers. Check the requirements of each university carefully if in doubt.'
>
> An admissions tutor for economics

Your predicted grades are very important and your tutor at school and subject staff are responsible for these. They will base their predictions on your class tests and mock examinations, as well as on other considerations such as your attitude to study, attendance, punctuality and so forth. They are, however, predictions and only you honestly know what is realistic. Your GCSE, or equivalent, results are also important because these are an actual record of past performance. If the predictions for your A levels appear very optimistic compared to your past performance then universities may well be sceptical of the likelihood of you attaining these predictions. If you are worried about this then it may be best to wait to defer your application until after you have received your A level results. This may mean waiting another year before starting your degree, although there are ways you can make a late application through UCAS – check their website for details.

There is always, of course, an element of chance involved in all of this. For example, you may be made a conditional offer and still be accepted even if you drop a grade.

Academic excellence and employment prospects

Academic excellence

The quality and nature of teaching and assessment is an important consideration when choosing your university. As mentioned earlier, in England the Office for Students is responsible for monitoring the quality of degrees through the Teaching Excellence Framework, and their website may help you with your choices.

For universities across the UK, the *Guardian* (www.guardian.com/education/universityguide) and the *Times* (www.thetimes.co.uk) provide useful information about university league tables and subject rankings. Please note that the *Times* can only be accessed via a subscription.

The library

The library is a far more important part of university life than you might imagine. You may need sources that cannot leave the building and when it comes to revision the library is quiet, warm and a place to escape from house-mates when you need 'me-time'. Many students find their own special place in the library where they go to work and some university libraries cater for all preferences with open tables, closed booths and secret corners. Some libraries are very inspiring with domes and ancient tomes; others are temples of chrome and glass. Of course, online access to resources is important, but do check out the library. Some Open Day tours will miss out the library – insist on seeing it and ask about opening hours. Some libraries are open all night to cater for the night owls.

> **TIP!**
>
> You know best how easy or difficult you find academic study. If you are accepted onto a very academic course that doesn't really suit, you may struggle and may be unhappy.

Employment prospects

While your time at university is a time to become independent, have new experiences and make new friends, it is also the next step in your education. The expectation is that it will lead to more opportunities in the labour market than if you did not complete a degree. In 2013, the Department for Business, Innovation and Skills of the UK government claimed that, over a lifetime, male graduates in the UK would earn £170,000 more than male non-graduates and female graduates would earn £250,000 more than female non-graduates. However, this claim is very difficult to verify because there are so many variables to consider; and, as all economists know, there are 'three types of lies; lies, damn lies and statistics' (attributed to Disraeli 1804–81).

Nevertheless, you should think seriously about life after you complete your education and what you want from your degree. You must look very closely at the university prospectuses to see what they say about future employment prospects and whether or not these jobs are considered graduate-level jobs. Consider also how much support the university might be able to offer when you are job-hunting; some university lecturers are very difficult to extract references from whereas others are very helpful.

The website www.graduate-jobs.com lists job opportunity by employment sector.

A WORD OF CAUTION: Unlike your education to date, your degree has a not inconsiderable price-tag and it will be YOUR debt not your parents'. The price is the same whether you work hard and use all the opportunities that are available at university or whether you do not.

Non-academic considerations

Location

You are committing three years of your life to this place; you have to know if this is somewhere that you will feel happy and safe living. Everyone feels at least a little homesick when starting university; you may have had the same circle of familiar faces around you since you were in primary school! Overseas students and those who have been to boarding school will find some aspects of this easier than the majority of students, but conversely they may find other aspects harder.

For a small group of islands, the cultural and climatic variations within the UK are enormous. Leeds is very different from Exeter, as is Aberystwyth from Kent. Some of you will want to experience the buzz of big city life; others will be more comfortable in a small town. As a first step, think about where you have visited that you liked, talk to friends and family, research the area around the different universities and beware stereotypes! The 'North' is not all *Coronation Street* and London is neither *EastEnders* or *Made in Chelsea*. Go travelling, explore – don't just go on Open Days.

Accessibility is another factor. Some of you may be desperate to get as far from home as possible; just make sure that you can return easily for those all-important school reunions and home-cooked meals! If you drive and have your own car; is there somewhere safe to keep it at university? How long will the journey take and how much will it cost?

Cost of living

The cost of university is more than just your tuition fees. You have accommodation, food, text books, travel and maybe even an occasional night out to budget for. These costs are sometimes hidden in the depth of a university's website so you need to look closely. There are some excellent apps to help you budget, but you need to know what the bottom line is.

Student accommodation is of a much higher quality now than it was in the past but those study bedrooms with en suite facilities come at a price. Some accommodation providers expect you to pay full rent during the holidays; others use the accommodation for conferences during the holidays so you have to clear your stuff. You need to know these details and look at the total annual cost of the accommodation. Surprisingly, some of the regional universities have more expensive accommodation than some of the London colleges when you look at annual costs versus weekly costs.

Research also the price of student rental properties other than halls of residence. Most students have to live 'out' for at least one year. Is a house easy to find? Are there areas of town that may be affordable but where you may not feel safe living? If you have to pay for taxis rather than walking it could add considerably to your costs.

In many countries around the world students tend not to travel away to study but go to their local university and live at home with family. The amount you could save this way may balance the differences in course content between the local university and a distant alternative. Economists are familiar with the concept of 'opportunity cost' (in this case, a benefit missed when an individual chooses one alternative over another), and writing a long list of the costs and benefits of each university may be a wise move at this point.

Campus or town?

Some UK universities were established on campuses: relatively closed and compact sites where the accommodation blocks, lecture theatres, administration blocks, laboratories, library and all the other teaching, leisure and sport facilities are together. This can be very convenient and helps you form close friendships and feel very safe on campus. It may, however, lead to a separation between 'town and gown' that means you are not part of the wider community.

Some urban universities still manage to have a semi-campus feel that may be a satisfactory compromise – such as the cluster of institutions in London around University College London. Student accommodation may not necessarily be on a campus as such but the community in halls may resemble a campus in many ways with social events and a bar.

The choice of 'campus or not' is a personal one and probably ought not to be as important a consideration as some of the others. I'd recommend talking to students you meet at Open Days; ask them what they like most and least about their university.

Case studies

Clive studied economics in a big city and spent his first year in student accommodation some distance from the university. He quickly became used to cycling everywhere and loved all the opportunities to attend live music events in a vibrant and exciting cultural centre.

Lily studied management with accounting at a small university with a very beautiful campus in a rural area. She loved her accommodation, which was grand and reeked of history, and she loved being within a short walking distance of the lecture theatre. However, she found it very quiet at weekends because many of the students went home to their families or visited friends elsewhere.

Frances studied economics at a big city university with a lovely landscaped campus within easy reach of the city centre. She threw herself into student life; took a part-time job in the student bar, was elected onto the Student Union and learnt to sail with the university sailing club – a hobby she has kept up on graduation.

Friends and family

Your parents/guardians are stakeholders in your education and will want to be involved in your decision making. And these days universities make an astonishing effort to woo parents/guardians rather than the potential students, offering the likes of sample lectures and some heavy marketing. Your parents/guardians may also be making a financial contribution to your living costs, so please don't shut them out!

If you think your parents/guardians are trying to influence your choices remind them (gently) that you are your own person with your own preferences and that you must make your own choices. The same applies to any pressure to follow a family tradition.

Friends may also be influential in decision making; this is difficult to avoid. However, you will not be the same person at 21 that you were at 18 and you must put your own education and future career before personal friendships. True friendship survives being apart.

4| The UCAS application

The following advice should help you complete your UCAS application. More specific advice on filling in your application is given in *How to Complete Your UCAS Application* (Trotman Education), which is updated annually. This chapter is designed to reinforce your school programme, as well as to give extra help to those who may not have the support of their schools.

The application form

Most schools spend time in the final term of Year 12 and the first term of Year 13 supporting the UCAS process. There will be an experienced teacher overseeing the process, and in PSHE (Personal Social and Health Education) lessons you will probably be offered talks and workshops to help you get started. You will also be given a UCAS 'buzzword' that you will need to use to register on the UCAS website. If you are applying as an individual, maybe if you are a mature student, you can register without a buzzword, but they will need to ask you a few more questions. It is advisable to get started on the application as quickly as possible; it is far more time consuming than many students realise. Once you're registered you can log on and work on your application whenever you like, and you can save changes as you go along. The UCAS website itself is very helpful: www.ucas.com/undergraduate/applying-university/filling-your-ucas-undergraduate-application. The whole form is completed electronically through their website www.ucas.com/students.

Getting started

1. Personal information

The first section is the most straightforward because you ought to know your own personal information! There are questions, some of which are optional, that ask for information about whether you have been in care, special needs, criminal convictions, etc. Some of this information is shared with your chosen universities before they offer you a place, and some after. Above all, be honest.

2. Student finance

There is a short student finance section. Universities want to know who is going to pay your fees. UCAS uses this section to help you to apply for funding; unless you are self-financing. Student loans are arranged through your local authority but the application form is also filled in online at www.gov.uk/apply-online-for-student-finance. NB: This process doesn't start until you've confirmed your offer.

3. Your choices of university

This section is where you enter your choices of university courses. Check the course codes carefully – you don't want to make the mistake of applying for anthropology in Aberystwyth when you intended to apply for business in Aberdeen!

When you make your choices you will put in the year of entry (that means the year that you want to start your course). The majority of students go straight to university the autumn after they leave school but some will choose deferred entry; this means that they want to wait a year before starting their course and are planning a gap year.

Deferred entry

Deferred entry is not a decision to take lightly but there can be work experience advantages to taking a planned gap year, as mentioned in Chapter 2. Be aware though that planned Gap Year adventures with Gap Year travel specialists may reveal more about your socio-economic background than they do about your thirst for adventure.

Some courses do not allow deferred entry so please check the prospectus carefully, as it would look odd if you applied to be deferred for some courses but not for all. The reasons for the deferred entry and your gap year plans must be discussed in your personal statement.

There is risk in applying for deferred entry. If you are applying for a very competitive course then you are competing against not just your current year group but also those following on in the year below. Unless you are an outstanding student with fantastic references, high predicted grades and have already got a very interesting gap year plan finalised, then you are probably best advised not to defer. If you are deferring because school is hard work and you fancy a break, then universities will not be in a hurry to welcome you on to their course.

If you were considering deferring because you are anxious about your A level results, then it may be better to wait a year before starting your application. Your school may not like this because of the extra administration supporting you after you have officially left school; however, most schools will be supportive, especially if you discuss it fully in advance with your form tutor.

4. Education

The Education section is the one where the most mistakes are made. You may know that you have GCSE French – but do you know which exam board set the paper? You must also add all the examination units that you are going to sit in the future. Before you start this section, find all your certificates and statements of results. These are very important documents and should be kept safely with your birth certificate and other important personal documentation. Employers may want to see original certificates for exams, even when you're close to retirement age! Get used to keeping them safe. If you have a problem with finding your past examination results – **DO NOT LEAVE IT UNTIL THE LAST MINUTE** – follow it up with the school where you sat the exam as they will keep records, even if you left some time ago. Contact the examinations officer not the subject staff. If you are at the same school your form teacher should be able to help you, although it may take some time. It is an offence to miss out results that you do not like very much. If you have results you are ashamed of, discuss them in the personal statement rather than attempt to hide anything. Other types of examinations, such as practical music and dance qualifications, can also be included; the UCAS website has details on this.

5. Employment

There is a section for your employment history. If you completed your schooling some years ago then the universities want to know how you have been spending your time. This section is only for **paid** work; you can add any part-time jobs, casual holiday work and Saturday jobs, but not unpaid internships, work-experience schemes or cash-in-hand family tasks. You can discuss the latter in your personal statement.

6. Personal statement

When you have completed these sections then you can upload your personal statement into the space provided. You should have been working on this for some time – only upload the finished article. See Chapter 5 for more information on the personal statement.

7. Reference

The final Reference section will be completed, in most cases, by your school. This is your academic reference and it will also include your predicted grades. If you have not filled in the Education section correctly then your referee will be unable to enter predicted grades. If you have been out of school for some time and have not started your application with your education centre's 'buzzword', then you will be able to choose your own referee. This needs to be someone who can comment with authority on your suitability to follow a course of academic study. It may be an employer or a family friend or former teacher, but whoever it is can only be your referee if they know how you have spent your time between further education and applying for higher education. Make sure you ask well in advance of the UCAS deadline.

Schools and colleges take their references and predicted grades very seriously because they have their own reputations to consider. Most schools and colleges will also go through your whole application with a fine-tooth comb to ensure that every section is accurate and that there are no errors of spelling or grammar.

The tutor who is responsible for your reference will ask your subject teachers and anyone else you work with in sport or extra-curricular activities, for their input. Their reference will also include details of academic prizes you have won and other honours such as sports colours or being a senior prefect. This means that you don't have to mention these in your personal statement. It is your responsibility to ensure that your tutor knows about all of these awards, so make sure that you attend all tutor appointments and attend prepared to provide evidence.

The academic reference usually starts with a paragraph common to all applicants that gives the school or college context, such as average GCSE scores, the number of students that qualify for free school meals and maybe the nature of the school catchment area. This helps the university assess your academic potential and may lead to what is called a **contextual offer** that may be lower than their standard offer.

The reference will also comment on your attendance and punctuality. If there are personal circumstances that you would like the university to be aware of then make sure that your tutor knows to do this. The converse is also true, i.e. if you would rather some personal details were not disclosed. Your reference will never be negative; your tutor is obliged to show you in a positive light, so please do not be anxious about that. Universities are very good at reading 'between the lines' though, so it is advisable to complete all those homework assignments and meet all deadlines from your very first day on the A level course!

Finally, remember that it is *your* reference: ask to see it before it is uploaded. If there are parts that you do not like then you can request to have it modified. Your referee will not tell lies on your behalf but you can negotiate to soften or strengthen aspects of the reference.

Finally: **submit and pay!** This is the moment you have been waiting for. But do not expect klaxons. UCAS won't receive your reference until your school or college is completely satisfied, and that usually means that you have paid the fee and they have checked the whole application carefully. If your school or college collects your payment directly from you, rather than as part of a school fee, do not leave it until the last minute. Pay when you start the process, not at the end. You do not want any delays after all your hard work!

What to expect next

You will receive an email acknowledgement from UCAS. Make sure that UCAS emails are delivered into your inbox not spam folders. There is also the opportunity to **Track** your application through the UCAS Track facility.

If you have made an application to Oxford or Cambridge (Oxbridge) you will need to make the arrangements to do the pre-interview assessments; your school or college will help you with this, and you will need to have submitted your application at an earlier date (October) than the standard deadline.

There is always some discussion about whether or not it matters how early you submit your application. Some of the most competitive universities do not start looking at applications until early spring; other universities deal with all applications as they arrive in their system from UCAS.

In general, universities look at applications in several stages. The first step will be to check that you meet their entrance criteria; it is only after that stage that admissions tutors will look at items such as your personal statement.

Universities are unlikely to contact you directly; they work through UCAS and UCAS will pass their responses on to you. There are three possible responses that you may receive and you don't need to do anything; at least until you have heard back from all of your choices.

1. **A conditional offer.** This means that your place is there if you attain the grades that the university is asking for. These are usually the expected grades as outlined in the prospectus, but some applicants may receive a conditional offer that is a little lower if the university feels that you are a particularly 'good fit' for their course; maybe because you have other attributes and experience. Although it is not unheard of for students to be made very high conditional offers.

2. **An unconditional offer.** These are usually made to applicants who have already completed their A level or equivalent courses and received their results. However, in recent years these have been increasingly (and controversially) given to students who have not completed their schooling. In 2018, UCAS reported that 23% of students received at least one unconditional offer. Unconditional offers are unpopular with subject teachers as they think that students may stop trying to do so well in their courses. And employers have voiced concerns that they may not be able to judge candidates effectively if many people are accepted to university with unconditional offers. In response, some universities have announced that they are not going to make this type of unconditional offer in the

future. UCAS themselves advise applicants to be very cautious about accepting these offers.

After you have received offers from your chosen universities you have to make a commitment. You are allowed to accept two conditional offers – one as '**firm**' and one as '**insurance**'. The insurance choice really ought to be an offer that is lower than your firm choice, so that you still have a place even if you do not attain your predicted grades. The situation for unconditional offers is slightly different; applicants may be made unconditional offers on the condition that they make this their firm choice. If you receive unconditional offers it is recommended that you discuss these with your tutor in school; the UCAS website provides excellent guidance, too.

3. **A rejection.** This will be disappointing, but if you have made one or two aspirational choices then you must be prepared for some disappointment. If you have been rejected by all your universities you may need to take stock, but do not despair. At this point you could consider making one extra application through **UCAS Extra**. UCAS Extra is for applicants who have either rejected all their offers or been rejected by all five. This service usually becomes available on the UCAS website in February, and you will be able to check through UCAS as to which universities may still have vacancies on their courses. Further to this, your final option is to wait until **Clearing** opens on results day, which again allows you to search for courses with vacancies.

For further information on Clearing, see Chapter 8 – Results day.

Your role at this point is to work hard on your assignments and revision so that you attain the best possible results. This is a time for focus. Imagine you're an elite athlete and train your mind and body: eat healthy food, forget the parties and consider stopping any part-time work. Your priority now are your A levels.

Entrance examinations and other tests

The UCAS website has a list of all the different institutions and any entrance or aptitude tests they ask for as part of their admissions requirements. A close look at this list indicates that, with the exceptions of the universities of Oxford and Cambridge, tests for economics and business courses are only required to support non-standard applications; these tests are often to assess English language skills in overseas applicants. See Chapter 7 – Non-standard applications.

The University of Cambridge has standardised pre-interview assessments for many subjects, including economics courses. There are two papers.

1. An 80-minute mathematics test. This is designed to be very challenging, and all Cambridge colleges expect an A grade at A level (or equivalent) Mathematics.

2. A 40-minute extended writing task. No prior knowledge of economics is expected, but the written test will have an economics 'theme'. You are provided with some stimulus material for you to read and then complete a task based on this material. In the university's words: 'Your answer will be assessed taking into account your ability to construct a reasoned, insightful and logically consistent argument with clarity and precision.' Some colleges also ask for one or two essays that you have written in school. They like to see how your teacher has assessed your work so you must talk to your teachers about this; it doesn't have to be an economics essay. More information about the entrance tests can be found at www.admissionstesting.org/for-test-takers/cambridge-pre-interview-assessments.

Related courses that you may be interested in at the University of Cambridge are land economy and management studies. Land economy applicants must take a Thinking Skills Assessment test: a 90-minute paper covering critical thinking and problem solving. Details of this are also on the website mentioned above. Management studies is only open to students who have already completed two or three years on any degree course at Cambridge.

You will be asked to sit a Thinking Skills Assessment paper if you are interested in economics, management or PPE courses at the University of Oxford. This follows the same format as the Cambridge test above but also sets a 30-minute extended writing task; there is a choice of three essay questions on general subjects that do not require any specialised knowledge. More information about these tests, including past papers to practise, are available at www.admissionstesting.org/for-test-takers/thinking-skills-assessment/tsa-oxford/about-tsa-oxford.

When Oxford and Cambridge decide who to offer places to, they take these tests into account as well as your written UCAS application (including personal statement and school reference), plus the candidate's performance at interview.

Suggested timeline

GCSE results day

Look at your results and think about your strengths and weaknesses. Think also about what sorts of careers interest you so that you make the best possible choices regarding the next steps in your post-16 education. For example, depending on your result, ought you to consider re-taking GCSE Mathematics? Resolve to work hard. **And put those results slips somewhere safe!**

Year 12

Summer term

- Your tutors and PSHE staff will start talking about university applications. Take these sessions seriously and listen to advice. Discuss your options with your friends and at home. Ask everyone and anyone what they think and try to visit some university towns and campuses.
- Have a look on the UCAS and Office for Students websites.
- Browse the prospectuses and other brochures in your school or college library or careers library.
- Chat to your subject staff and make sure you do well in any summer exams so that they are confident to predict you good grades.
- Make a start gathering the information that will help you write your personal statement.

Summer holiday

- Try to get work experience, as discussed in Chapter 2.
- Research the universities that you are interested in – as well as some you're not. Make sure that you really want to go to particular universities by considering the alternatives.
- Read around your subjects. University departments often post suggested reading lists on their website for prospective applicants.
- Broaden your horizons with theatre trips and visits to museums and art galleries. Get out of your comfort zone and challenge yourself. You may be surprised.
- If you have the option to travel try to visit places that are less well-known and see if you can experience local life as well as the tourist trail.

Year 13

September

- Get started on that UCAS application. Register on the website and enter your personal details. This will make your tutor happy if nothing else!
- Get your personal statement under way.

October

- The Oxbridge deadline.
- Enter your education and examination results to date on to your application.

- Consider Open Days.
- Talk to your subject teachers about your predicted grades.

November

- Make your choices and enter them on to the application.
- Complete your personal statement.
- Pre-interview assessments for Oxbridge.

December

- Finalise your application, and submit.
- If you're lucky you may get your first offer before Christmas!

Spring term

- Track your application.
- Go to any Open Days organised for successful applicants.
- Think about which places will be your firm and insurance choices.
- Do not lose your nerve if you've not heard anything yet. No news is good news.
- Consider UCAS Extra if necessary.
- Revise for your mock examinations; even if you've got offers, the hardest work is still to come.

After Easter

- Apply for student finance if required.
- Dream about what you're going to do with your time after your last exam is over – and maybe look for a summer job.
- Finalise your firm and insurance choices with UCAS.
- Revision, revision, revision.

August

- EXAMINATION RESULTS!

5 | The personal statement

The personal statement is your opportunity to convince your chosen universities that they want **you**. It is your vehicle to market yourself and, as such, it is possibly the most important part of the application. You have a maximum of 47 lines – about 4,000 characters – to do this. **Every word must count**. As a consequence of this, most students are naturally very hesitant about starting their personal statement.

The key word is **personal**. Do not be tempted to copy online personal statements and do not convince a relative, however articulate they may be, to write it for you. Admissions tutors claim they can tell immediately if the statement has been written by someone aged around 18 or by someone middle-aged. Ultimately, it is **your personality** that needs to shine through.

How to start

You are going to write lots of notes and then lots of drafts of your personal statement, so the sooner you start the better.

Why you want to study business and/or economics

Begin by jotting down your thoughts about *why* you want to study business and/or economics-related subjects. Be honest! Is it because you want a well-paid and secure job in the future? That is nothing to be ashamed of – so say so. But also say how your selected course could help you on your way.

You will not have had a passion for accounts from an early age and no toddler is fascinated by the workings of the stock exchange. Those are the types of statements that cause admissions tutors to roll their eyes – 'passion' is a word to avoid. On the other hand, it is certainly possible that as a small child you enjoyed playing shop and handling money; maybe you have relatives who have their own business and you helped them from when you were quite young.

Or, perhaps you were introduced to the subject area more recently; maybe you were inspired by a TED talk or a TV personality, or perhaps an event in the local or global economy that sparked your interest, or perhaps something a teacher said or a particular topic in your A level course was your trigger. These are all valid reasons for choosing business and economics. Whatever your sparking point, just make sure you can fully justify your choice of subject.

WORD OF WARNING!

Some students like to start with a quote – maybe from Adam Smith, Karl Marx or Warren Buffett. This could be a risky strategy but, if it reflects your personality and is not too quirky, then that is your choice.

The next step

Why you have chosen this course

Every university is proud of their courses and they want to know why you chose them over the competition. This is perhaps a little more tricky because you are applying for five courses that will all have slight differences. It is unwise to apply to more than one course at the same university, especially if they are very different from each other. If an admissions tutor is selecting students for an economics degree course, he or she will be looking for personal statements that address economics; if an admissions tutor is selecting students to study business studies, he or she will be expecting to read about business-related issues. It is important, therefore, to ensure that there is as much compatibility between your five choices as possible, otherwise you run the risk of being rejected by all of them.

Look closely at the individual prospectuses. Pick out the common themes and topics that particularly interest you and that you are keen to investigate in greater detail. Perhaps you read a book or article that relates to these or perhaps you were involved in something during work experience that provided a platform to build further study onto. It could be that you are enthusiastic about opportunities to spend time abroad as part of the course; what would you hope to gain from that? There is nothing wrong with recognising that there are problems in the world and that your university course may give you the tools to start exploring possible solutions. You could say where and when you became aware of issues that interest you. Was it the experience of a friend or relative? Was it from observing traders in developing countries? Was it a news item about a lack of resources in an essential service?

'To study management, you need to demonstrate that you are capable of managing yourself. Your personal statement needs to be structured, organised and free of spelling or grammatical errors. You should aim to be unique and original and provide a good opening line that reveals something about your aptitude and enthusiasm. I really like to see statements that demonstrate personality and flair but don't go too over the top. Keep it formal and remain objective. I am impressed by applicants who describe situations where they've demonstrated relevant skills, such as good communication or teamwork, problem-solving, initiative, leadership or achieving goals.'

Admissions tutor, University of Suffolk

Explain how your choice of A levels support your choice of degree

All your subjects are contributing to developing your skill set and it is important to identify the skills that are transferable into the next level of your education.

You need to include a paragraph about your A levels, or equivalent, starting with any subjects that the universities specifically mention in their entrance requirements for the courses you are applying to with any facilitating subjects you are studying (see page 30). There is no need to tell the admissions officer details about the syllabus as they are already familiar with this. Focus on the skills; perhaps you write essays, give presentations, spend time on independent study, use data and manipulate statistics or have to follow instructions closely. These are the sort of skills that the university wants to know about.

Universities want to know that if you take a place with them you will be hard-working, conscientious, know how to learn and able to meet deadlines. So show that you can! Provide evidence – there is no point in making unsupported assertions. When, where and how did you display these skills?

This section of the personal statement will be mirrored by your tutor reference so that the two parts of your application support each other. So you must work closely with the person writing that reference; you must avoid contradicting each other.

If you are studying for an Extended Project Qualification (EPQ) then it is worth highlighting this because of the independent research and time-management skills that it requires. Your EPQ may be the factor that determines whether or not you are offered a place, particularly if you are a mathematics plus further mathematics student.

Academic interest

As a rule of thumb about 65% to 75% of your personal statement needs to have an academic slant. You need to prove that you are interested in the particular courses that you are applying for. The best students read around their subjects and find connections between their subjects and the wider world. For example, an business student may find a journal article about the economic impacts of climate change. Admissions tutors like to see evidence that you read and that your television viewing extends beyond soaps and fantasy dramas. Admissions tutors want to know where you stand, and why, on the big issues of the day.

Discuss books, articles or documentaries that have interested you. Avoid explaining the content to the reader – you must never teach the teacher! Comment on what stuck in your mind from reading it, then link this to what you hope to explore further through your selected course or what might add to your knowledge or give you an alternative perspective.

It's also a good idea to try and research the staff at your chosen institutions, and maybe read some of their published works – or certainly works with a similar theme. If you found a book very difficult to read; that is also fine, and you can say so. You are not expected to be the 'finished product' yet; after all, you are going to university to learn! It is also acceptable to 'dip in' to a book, just do not pretend that you read it all.

In this section of the statement you should also mention lectures or conferences that you have attended, and recount any particularly memorable speakers or ideas heard; particularly if they caused you to challenge prior held beliefs.

Universities are looking for students that they will enjoy working with; students who are keen to learn and receptive to new ideas. They want students who are **teachable**. They do not want to work with students who know it all already. Therefore, be modest, and focus on what you want to learn rather than what you know already.

'This is not the place to list your A levels and what you've done in them. It is also not the place to try and link everything to economics, especially if the link is tenuous. Try and avoid saying "Studying English literature has improved my essay-writing skills and helped me construct concise arguments" or "Mathematics has helped with my data analysis skills". This is self-evident and a waste of characters. Instead, talk about specific topics in your studies (related to economics) that have particularly interested you and why. Don't just explain what different areas of economics are about – admissions tutors will be familiar with the concepts you're talking about – rather reflect on them. While you want to present your-self as a good economics student, if your personal statement becomes simply a short essay about economics or a particular theory or concept then it's saying nothing about you as a person.'

An admissions tutor for economics

Extra-curricular activities

Any extra-curricular activities you participate in will have provided you with skills such as cooperation, teamwork, dedication, the ability to recover from disappointment and resilience. Consequently there may follow a paragraph about activities such as sport, Combined Cadet Force, Duke of Edinburgh, music and drama. While these may help you to stand out against your competition, they may also say more about your socio-economic background and your school's facilities than it does about your determination and commitment. Any opportunities that you have been able to create for yourself are more impressive than those that are an everyday part of your school or college life. Consider mentioning achievements where you were up against a lot of competi-tion. There is probably not a lot of point in mentioning activities prior to sixth form either unless they are particularly noteworthy.

Do not worry unduly if you have little to say here. Some of you may have long journeys to school or college and family commitments that make additional activities difficult; and many of you may prefer reading a book to running about on a sports field. The Cambridge scholar Dame Mary Beard commented recently along the lines that she enjoys teaching more now that Cambridge is no longer a place for students with one eye on the rugby pitch or on the boathouse!

Gap years - both intentional and unintentional!

If you are in the position of re-taking and re-applying you can turn this into a positive. You could discuss your disappointment with your grades and how determined you are not to repeat the same mistakes. This additional year can also be an opportunity to learn more about your chosen future line of work by finding part-time work or an internship. And you may even be able to find the time to tackle that pile of unread *The Economist* magazines!

Remember, however, that some universities prefer you to gain all your qualifications at once and others do make higher offers than standard to re-sit students. Check the prospectus very carefully and contact the admissions department directly to find out how this may affect you.

Intentional gap years fall into two groups – those that are planned around deferred entry and those taken by students who did not want to make an application before they got their A level results. In either case, talk about how you plan to spend your time and how this will make you a better student in the future. If you are already working, you can discuss the skills you are learning from being in employment, such as reliability and punctuality. Applying after you have your results does have some benefits: the university knows exactly what your educational attainment is and so they may prefer to make you an offer rather than an applicant who is still untested.

The personal

You are an individual; there is no one else quite like you, so let your personality shine through. Do not pretend to be someone who you believe admissions tutors might prefer. Write fluently and in your own words – not slang of course, this is a formal exercise; but do not write as if you were born in the 1940s. Do not use words that you have never used before and will never use again; if you do, your statement will not sound natural. Let it be your authentic voice! It is recommended to read your statement aloud to family members one by one. That way you can see if it flows and you can judge by their reactions if you have done a good job or if you are coming across as fake.

Include personal information about you and your family. For example, if you are the first person in your family to go to university or if you spent your early years living in a different country, say so. Make these experiences relevant to your choice of subject and course. These little facts make you stand out and may make all the difference.

One student, as a small child, nearly drowned in a flood in Bangladesh. He was rescued by a local beggar and returned to his family who rewarded the beggar by giving him a home with them. This had a profound impact on the boy who consequently wanted to study development economics and work in flood prevention. One university emailed his referee to confirm the truth of the story, then went on to make a very attractive contextual offer. The young man hadn't wanted to tell the story on his application; he was embarrassed. He had to be convinced that it was a splendid use of available characters! Incidentally, Adam Smith (1723–90, a founding father of modern economics) was apparently kidnapped by tinkers as a child and rescued by his uncle.

How to finish

This can feel as difficult as getting started! However, you want the statement to read as a complete document and not just stop abruptly, so you need a conclusion.

At this point, write something that sums up your love for your subject and conveys your enthusiasm to get started on your university course.

Language

Given the limit on the number of characters (4,000) that make up the personal statement, it is important to make every sentence count, and not to waste space with passages that are at best too general and at worst meaningless.

Use clear, simple English and make sure that the content of what you are writing impresses the selectors, rather than trying to win them over with flowery, overcomplicated phrases.

> *'I was privileged to be able to undertake some work experience with a well-known high-street bank where I was able to see the benefit of having the ability to be confident with information technology.'*
>
> **– 199 characters**

This could be rewritten as:

> *'My three-week work placement at HSBC showed me the importance of being proficient in using spreadsheets.'*
>
> **– 106 characters**

Similarly:

> *'I was honoured to be able to captain my school Under-14, Under-15, Second XV and First XV rugby sides, and from this I learnt how to be an effective leader and an excellent communicator.'*
>
> **– 186 characters**

… could be rewritten as:

> *'Captaining my school 1st XV taught me the importance of strong leadership and communication skills.'*
>
> **– 99 characters**

Phrases to avoid include the following.

- 'I was honoured to be …'
- 'I was privileged to …'

- 'From an early age ...'
- 'It has always been my dream to ...'

Sample personal statements

Sample personal statement 1 (character count: 1,605)

I have chosen to study management at university because I want to run a business in the future, and management skills will be very important for this. I first became interested in management because my father runs a company and so I was able to see how important this aspect of the business is.

Last summer, I spent two weeks shadowing a department manager in a local company, and I gained an insight into the skills required to be a successful manager. In particular, I observed the need for good communication skills. I enjoy reading *The Economist* and the business sections of the national newspapers.

I am studying mathematics, economics and physics at A level. Mathematics is useful because it helps me to understand balance sheets and share prices, which are essential skills for a successful businessman. Economics has taught me how a company's success depends on how it adapts to the way the market is performing, and how it copes with fluctuations in the global economy. Physics teaches me how to be analytical and how to solve problems.

At school, I am captain of the 1st XV rugby team. This requires the ability to show leadership qualities and to manage people. It also allows me to get rid of stress. I play the trombone in the school orchestra, which involves teamwork and manual dexterity. I like reading, going to the cinema and photography. I also have a passion for opera. On Saturdays, I work at the local Louisiana Fried Turkey fast-food restaurant, and so I have gained excellent communication and teamwork skills. In my gap year I hope to travel and to gain more work experience.

Points raised by sample personal statement 1

- It is too short, at fewer than 2,000 characters (remember the maximum is 4,000 characters). You should aim to use the full amount of space available.

- Although the candidate has addressed all of the relevant issues, there is a lack of detail. It is too general and tells us very little about the candidate.
- It is not very personal.

An admissions tutor's comments on sample personal statement 1

'I have chosen to study management at university because I want to run a business in the future, and management skills will be very important for this.' (1) 'I first became interested in management because my father runs a company' (2) 'and so I was able to see how important this aspect of the business is.' (3)

1. Why are management skills important? Give an example of a situation you have seen, discussed or read about that illustrates this.
2. Give details of the company. What does it do? Who does it trade with?
3. An example would add detail to this section – perhaps recount an incident that shows the importance of a good management structure, or about the need to delegate.

'Last summer, I spent two weeks shadowing a department manager' (4) 'in a local company,' 'and I gained an insight into the skills required to be a successful manager. In particular, I observed the need for good communication skills.' (5) 'I enjoy reading The Economist *and the business sections of the national newspapers.' (6)*

4. Which department? What did the company do? How big was it? You could write something along the lines of '… which manufactured electric motors to be used in agricultural settings …' This might well stimulate an interesting discussion at the interview stage.
5. Give an example, such as 'As an example of this, I remember one occasion when a local farmer needed us to adapt one of the products to …'
6. Also, give an example that relates to something you have studied at A level. This should be the strongest and longest section of the personal statement. I want to know much more about what the applicant gained from the work experience and why it has convinced him/her that my course is the right one.

'I am studying mathematics, economics and physics at A level. Mathematics is useful because it helps me to understand balance sheets and share prices, which are essential skills for a successful businessman. Economics has taught me how a company's success depends on how it adapts to the way the market is

performing, and how it copes with fluctuations in the global economy. Physics teaches me how to be analytical and how to solve problems.' (7)

7. This is OK, but could do with links between what the applicant has studied at A level and what he/she has discovered about business and management in the real world through reading and work experience.

'At school, I am captain of the 1st XV rugby team. This requires the ability to show leadership qualities and to manage people. It also allows me to get rid of stress. I play the trombone in the school orchestra, which involves teamwork and manual dexterity. I like reading, going to the cinema, and photography. I also have a passion for opera. On Saturdays, I work at the local Louisiana Fried Turkey fast-food restaurant, and so I have gained excellent communication and teamwork skills. In my gap year I hope to travel and to gain more work experience.' (8)

8. This sentence could be more detailed – rather than 'hope to travel', I would like to see something more definite – 'I have arranged to ...' I want to be reassured that the applicant is going to use the gap year wisely and to benefit from it.

Adding the extra information requested by this admissions tutor would add detail, make it more interesting for him to read (so he is more likely to want to meet the student), demonstrate that the student is interested enough in the subject to be thinking about links between his studies and his experiences, and bring the statement up to the required length.

Sample personal statement 2 was written by an international student who was subsequently offered places by all five of her chosen universities. It is very individual in style, and reflects the student's interest and achievements in mathematics, but, throughout, she relates mathematics to economics. Thus, she is able to demonstrate how one of her key strengths will be relevant to her university studies.

Sample personal statement 2 (character count: 3,938)

If mathematics uses numbers and symbols to convey ideas and concepts, and social sciences make use of language to express hypotheses, economics is something in between, since it requires not only the logical analysis of mathematics to address theoretical problems but also the clarity of language to convert its theoretical perspectives into real-world applications. It is this special feature of economics that initially drew my interest to the subject.

To understand more about economic models, I read *Fundamental Methods of Mathematical Economics* by Alpha Chiang. Although the methods and models described are at their simplest forms and not yet comprehensive enough to depict real-world problems, I was surprised to see how powerful mathematics can be in economics when different mathematical techniques, from the simple simultaneous equations and calculus that I have studied in A level Mathematics to complicated series expansions that I have not yet encountered, were employed in various micro and macro models to solve problems such as optimisation or national income. Knowing how powerful mathematics can be in economics, I'm also aware of its limitations. A model can be internally consistent but its subject matter, people, are capricious. This makes economic models sometimes unable to forecast events, such as recession. As such, economics is not independent of human psychology and we cannot study the subject in a vacuum.

In work-shadowing at the Finance Department of my province this summer, I found that statistics and econometrics in Vietnam have only been developed in the last two years. Indeed, our CPI (consumer price index) is calculated without weightings taken into account. This type of inaccuracy is quite common in Vietnam and draws a misleading picture of the economy's performance. I would like to pursue econometrics at university to help develop this branch of economics in my home country. I hope that with my contribution, no matter how small, Vietnam can produce reliable statistics and test economic policies on its own in the near future.

Coming from a developing nation, I cannot but have a strong interest in development economics. *Globalization and its Discontents* by Joseph Stiglitz has changed my view about the role of international economic institutions, particularly the IMF, in promoting economic welfare and stability. According to the author, the IMF is notorious in setting many conditions for its loans, and sometimes the loans made are insufficient or inefficient to help countries get out of predicaments. This also applies to Vietnam, when the IMF cut its loans for our poverty reduction programme in the three years to 2007, arguing that our central banks did not meet four of five criteria to qualify for the funding source. Having said that, since the book is eight years old, it fails to appreciate the efforts of the institution to make its fund more available to countries in need in recent years.

Outside of school, I enjoy solving maths puzzles and won a gold medal for the Senior Maths Challenge together with a distinction in the British Maths Olympiad. In Vietnam, I was also awarded fourth prize in the provincial maths competition for 11th grade gifted students when I was in my 10th grade, and the first prize in a maths contest for the 9th grade gifted students. In economics, I attended Target 2.0 last year. My group was in charge of the 'Cost and Price' section. This required dealing with figures such as commodity prices, input and output costs of firms, etc. and one must be able to choose the related data to make the rate decisions.

I enjoy reading novels in my free time; my favourite book is *Crime and Punishment*. Through reading, I have developed sympathy and moral concern towards the people and communities around me. I believe this to be an important virtue in an economist, because to understand people is the first condition for one to apply economics for the good of society.

General tips

- Before submitting your personal statement, ensure you check your application through very carefully for careless errors. Print a copy out to read through; it is harder to identify potential errors on a screen.
- Keep a copy of your personal statement so that you can remind yourself of what you have said, should you be called for interview.

And remember the seven rules for a successful application.

1. Research the course content.
2. Research the entrance requirements.
3. Find out your grade predictions.
4. Ensure your personal statement focuses on the course but remember to imagine how it will come across to each of the departments to which you are applying.
5. Include sufficient detail in the personal statement to make it stand out.
6. Illustrate your points with examples and evidence.
7. Every word in a personal statement counts, so don't use complicated language just to impress the admissions tutor.

6 | Succeeding at interview

Some universities will want to interview prospective students before making their final decisions, For example, the universities of Oxford and Cambridge will always interview before offering a place.

Success at interview is all about being prepared. As they say in business management – 'failing to prepare is preparing to fail'. However, the days of very harsh interviews where the interviewer is trying to catch the interviewee out are long gone. Employers and universities alike want to be seen as being welcoming and inclusive.

Planning in advance

Read through your application and your personal statement carefully.

The interviewer will have a copy of both documents in front of them and may well comment on points you have made in them, so you don't want to look surprised if they mention a book or event that you wrote about! If you have commented on books please make sure that you have read more than just an Amazon review; interviewers will know immediately if you are pretending.

You may have mentioned on your personal statement an event that sparked your interest in the subject and the interviewer may comment on this. Time will have passed since you wrote that statement. Harold Wilson said in 1964 'A week is a long time in politics'; and the same is certainly true in the political economy and in business. Make sure that you are aware of any developments that have happened since your chosen event – you will look a little foolish at interview if you have failed to notice something significant. This may also be an appropriate moment to ask the interviewer what their views are on your topic of interest.

Research the college and the course thoroughly

Make sure that you know what the main elements of the course are and have an idea about teaching methods and the expectations of the staff. You are likely to be interviewed by someone who may be teaching you, so look at a list of the faculty members and their specialisms. The lecturers may well have a Twitter presence, as they often use this platform to promote their own work, advertise lectures and link to articles and issues that they find interesting. If you are not yet following academics in areas that you're interested in on Twitter then now is definitely the time to start! Twitter is a very useful platform for news and current affairs, too.

Research the interview location

You may have to travel some distance so make sure you leave plenty of time and know exactly where you are going. You don't want to be late or flustered. Sometimes students will be asked to stay overnight. If you do stay overnight beware of having too much fun with the other interviewees; you never know who is watching. It is best to watch your language and table manners, too.

What are you going to wear?

Not a trivial question. You have to be comfortable and smart but you do not want to look like a 1950s bank manager. Most academics don't wear suits these days and even in the City very formal attire is unusual. Denim or sportswear, however designer, is probably too casual, but do not worry about revealing some of your personality in your choice of clothing or accessories. The interviewer will be assessing if you will fit into their establishment and whether or not you will be a pleasure to teach; first impressions are important. If you are happy in your choice of outfit then you will be confident and relaxed at interview; if your shoes are unfamiliar then you will be uncomfortable and miserable – and remember you will probably be taken on a walking tour at some point, too.

Practice interviews

If your school offers a practice interview please take advantage of the opportunity. If they do not, then talk to your subject teachers to see if they can arrange something. A practice interview will give you feedback about your posture, body language, volume of speech, speed of delivery and so forth. Beware: these practice sessions can often be more gruelling than the real thing!

Be well informed

Preparation for an interview should be an intensification of the work you are already doing outside class for your A level courses. Interviewers will be looking for evidence of an academic interest and commitment that extends beyond the classroom. They will also be looking for an ability to apply the theories and methods that you have been learning in your A level courses to the real world.

Whichever resources you use, this advice assumes that you will be taking a single honours business or management degree, but if you have chosen a joint or combined honours course you will have to prepare yourself for questions on those other subjects as well.

Either way, the interview is a chance for you to demonstrate knowledge of, commitment to and enthusiasm for business. The only way to do this is to be extremely well informed. Interviewers will want to know your reasons for wishing to study business. It is important to be aware of the many aspects of business, e.g. marketing, finance, personnel, and be clear about the differences between the various functions.

Be prepared to discuss current issues

Before your interview, it is vital that you are aware of current affairs related to the course for which you are being interviewed. Your interviewer may be interested in your views on what is happening in the 'real world' of business and economics. They might see this as an 'icebreaker' – a topic that you will be happy to discuss and will consequently relax you at the start so that your personality shines through. Remember, your interviewer is an expert; she or he will have a genuine passion for the subject and it will occupy a large part of their waking hours. They do not expect you to match them in expertise but they will expect some background knowledge. Therefore, make sure that you have seen some news before your interview date; make some rough notes that you can glance over as well. Speak to your subject teachers too, and don't forget Twitter! You should also keep up to date with current affairs in general.

Newspapers and magazines

As an A level student, you should already be reading a quality newspaper every day. The *Financial Times* will give you a good grasp of business, as will reading the business sections of the other broadsheets. Magazines are another important source of comment on current issues and deeper analysis. *The Economist* is a popular example, but you might also find it helpful to pick up a more specialist magazine such as *Talk Business*. Reading professionally written articles keeps you well informed about current events and gives you the chance to see how the vocabulary and language of business are used to communicate news and views. Magazines such as *Enterprise* and *HR* could also have some articles of interest to you. You do not have to buy all these – visit libraries or use the internet regularly to keep up to date with the business press. There are also subject-specific magazines such as Hodder Education's *Review* series, based around A level study. The interviewer does not have to have read the article you might mention, but it will show that you are 'reading around the subject' which is a key feature of the more able students.

Television and radio

It is also important to watch or listen to the news every day, again paying particular attention to business and economic news. Documentaries and programmes about the economy, business ventures, the politics of business and so on can be enormously helpful in showing how what you are studying is applied to actual situations and events. *Panorama* is a good example of the sort of television programme it would be useful to watch. *The Apprentice* and *Dragons' Den* can also be very informative.

Radio 4 offers *Money Box*, while the *Today* programme in the morning has up-to-the-minute reporting on economic and business develop-ments, often with interviews with those most closely involved. It is also a good idea to know the names of the chairman of the Confedera-tion of British Industry (CBI) and the governor of the Bank of England, for example, and the names of the country's top businesspeople. You can make a point of listening to what they have to say when they appear on *Question Time* or *Newsnight* on television, or *Any Questions* on Radio 4.

The internet

A wealth of easily accessible, continually updated and useful information is, of course, available on the internet. Given the ease with which infor-mation can be accessed, there is really no excuse for not being able to keep up to date with relevant current issues. YouTube and iTunes U gives free access to thousands of lectures and presentations from universities around the world; newspapers can be read online. In this age of information overload, anyone who is serious about keeping abreast of current issues has unlimited opportunities to do so. Thus, an interviewer is not going to be impressed with a student who claims he or she has been too busy to know what is happening in his or her chosen areas of interest.

The following could be particularly useful in your research.

- Subscribe to podcasts and download them regularly. BBC podcasts, which are free, include *Peter Day's World of Business, In Our Time, Money Box, Analysis, Start the Week* and *From Our Own Correspondent*.
- Check the BBC news website every day to see what news is breaking.
- If you can't buy a newspaper every day, then look at an online version.

Case study

'My first interview was a disaster. I had written about keeping up to date with current issues by reading *The Economist* and the second question they asked was about that week's edition. In fact, the last one I had read was three months before the interview. After that, they asked me about why I liked their course, and whether it differed in content from others I had applied for. What they really wanted to know was had I read their prospectus. I hadn't, and I got rejected.'

Michael, economics student

What to expect

Interviews vary and the term 'interview' may hide a lot of different activities, including group tasks and assessments. Your timetable for the day will tell you exactly what the format will be. There are 'rules' regarding interviews and all candidates are likely to be asked the same, or similar, questions. The days of weird and wonderful interviews have long passed. The interviewer will probably have a document that they will fill in as they talk to you.

'An interview is an opportunity for the applicant to communicate one-to-one with a member of staff, to know more about the university and the course.

'When an applicant is genuinely enthusiastic about their subject, their confidence is evident. It is important to gather their thoughts about why they are doing the course, what they want to achieve and why they have chosen our university.

'We want to understand the applicant's motivation, suitability for the course and what they want to achieve through the course. We may also check the applicant's experience according to their application. In terms of preparation, it would be useful for applicants to think about questions they want to ask and ensure they write these down in advance.'

Admissions tutor, Business Studies, University of Reading

The academic interview itself may be conducted by one person or by a panel. They will probably invite you to take a seat in a study and they may or may not be behind a desk. Try to maintain regular eye contact, although too much may be disconcerting. Be natural, watch the interviewer's face not just their eyes.

They will try to make you feel comfortable by asking you first about something they think you will be confident to discuss. You might be asked about an unusual prize you may have been awarded; try to be detailed and enthusiastic but don't ramble. Remember to smile.

You may well be asked to comment on something you wrote during the pre-interview assessment. Perhaps to develop or to explain a point you made in your extended writing. You are not expected to have much prior knowledge of very subject specific points but you are expected to have a solid general knowledge especially of current affairs.

They may ask you about something that you know very little about or that you are a little anxious about discussing. If you don't know an answer you must say so; don't make something up. If it is something you've not covered yet in class then say so. You could always turn the question around and ask them what they think. They are teachers, they like teaching, so ask them to explain something to you. They want you to be willing to learn and receptive to new ideas; they do not want to teach students who already think that they know everything and cannot listen. If they do talk at length then be attentive, don't fidget, smile and nod as appropriate.

Some interviewers will give you something to read prior to the interview and they will base the discussion around that. They are trying to assess your intellectual capabilities and how confident you are with new material. Try only to make points that you can back up with evidence; be evaluative and use reasoned judgement. Show that you can appreciate all sides of an argument but that you are prepared to reach a conclusion.

They may ask you if you have any questions. Try to avoid 'house-keeping' questions that are covered in the university prospectus. It is better to ask no questions than to say something just for the sake of it – especially if it's nearly lunch time! This could be your moment to ask a follow-up question about the interviewer's published work that you have read.

As you leave, remember to shake hands if offered and to say thank you. Try to be warm and friendly!

Likely interview questions

Questions may be straightforward and specific, but they can range to the vague and border on the seemingly irrelevant as well. Be prepared.

It is important to remember however, that you wouldn't have been invited for interview unless you were a serious candidate for a place on the course; so be confident and let your talents shine through.

Try practising your answers to the following questions.

Why have you chosen to study management?

Comment: Focus your answer to this question on how your studies and work experience have provided you with the motivation and interest to pursue this subject at university. This is an obvious starting point for your interviewers and they will probably want you to expand on the reasons for choosing your course that you highlighted in your personal statement. Assume that this question will arise and practise your answer to it: ensure that what you say is well structured and that you do not waffle – try to keep your answer relatively short and certainly no longer than two minutes.

Why do you want to study at this university?

Comment: This is another standard opening question and one that you should certainly be prepared for. You could talk about why the location of the university appealed to you, or how you were attracted to it via a personal recommendation. A prime factor that distinguishes one institution from another is the course it offers. You will need to ensure that you have researched the course in some depth to see what is studied and how it is organised and structured.

Why have you chosen these A levels?

Comment: You may apply for university degree courses that differ significantly from your subjects at A level. This will require an explanation. It does not kill your application – you would not be attending an interview if they were not willing to offer you a place – but it is a question that requires a proficient answer.

Have you visited here before?

Comment: If you have visited the university or attended an Open Day previously, this is your opportunity to mention it. Remember that the people conducting your interview will have contributed greatly to their department's Open Day and will welcome your feedback, but do keep it positive! Talk about it being a useful and informative occasion. Your interviewers will expect you to have done a lot of research into your chosen course and institution, so they will be expecting you to be well informed. (The university prospectuses and websites are good sources of information.) You do need to show that you are familiar with the particular institution to which you are applying. Answering this question by just saying 'No, but all universities are pretty much the same' will not improve your chances of getting a place.

What thoughts do you have on what you would like to do after you graduate?

Comment: Of course, you do not need to know exactly what career you would like to follow at the end of your degree at this stage – but you do need to have some thoughts on the kind of job you might be interested in. A possible answer might be: 'I would like a job that incorporates both my education and my practical skills: something combining my A level education with my working knowledge of customer service operations, entrepreneurial abilities and computer and administrative skills.' If, on the other hand, you do have a clear idea about what you would like to go into in the future, then talk about this – but remember to justify your reasons.

How do you think you are doing with your A levels?

Comment: The interviewer will know your predicted grades so you do not need to give too much information about these, but do state that you are working hard and making good progress. Talk about what topics you are studying at the moment and whether you are doing anything related to business and management. Elaborate on the aspects of the course you like, the skills you have gained and/or coursework projects where relevant. This is a relatively boring question, so take the opportunity to direct the conversation towards subjects that you are confident discussing and that will show you in the strongest light. Topics you are happy talking about should be prepared in advance.

What has attracted you to this course in particular?

Comment: This question, like the second one, enables you to show that you have thoroughly researched the particular course for which you are applying. You should draw on a particular aspect of the course that interests you and explain why. The university's website will generally give a precise breakdown of the core units that will be taught each year as well as the optional modules.

Tell me about any work experience you have had.

Comment: This is an important question. Expand on the description of work experience that you gave in your personal statement. Do not just list the things you saw and did – mention how you felt about and reacted to what you were seeing and doing. Did you enjoy it? Was there anything that particularly interested or surprised you? Try to give as personal an account as possible.

What are the main things you learned from your work experience?

Comment: This is another standard question that follows naturally from the preceding one. Talk about the varied nature of your experience. There might have been things that surprised you about the functioning of a business or about new technology that was used. How did it differ from your expectations? You could try to link this with things that you have been taught at A level if you have taken business studies, economics or accounting. Work experience includes any part-time or weekend jobs that you might have done. The interviewer will understand that the main reason that you have your Saturday job in a clothes shop is to earn some extra money, but they will be interested in seeing whether you have learned anything from it that might be relevant to your future degree studies. There are many opportunities to do this. Take the example of the clothes shop – you could discuss:

- whether the shop is part of a nationwide chain, or whether it is an independent business – and the advantages and disadvantages of each
- how the shop advertises and markets its range of clothing
- who the target buyers are, and how the business targets them
- how the goods are priced, and who the main competitors are
- the managerial structure of the shop
- the effects of a recession or an economic boom (whichever is relevant at the time of your interview)
- where the clothes are made, and the implications of this for the UK's economy
- customer relations.

How do you keep up to date with current developments in economics?

Comment: Economics (and business and management) issues change every day and to demonstrate a genuine interest in these subjects requires you to keep up to date with current developments. You need to read quality newspapers on a daily basis, watch the news and read specialist websites.

Have you followed any business cases in the news recently?

Comment: As mentioned, as an A level student, you should be reading a broadsheet newspaper every day. Talk about a recent article you have read and why you found it particularly interesting. This is another standard question and it is vital that you prepare your answer in advance. If you try to think of a topic off the top of your head without having given it any serious consideration previously, you could find that you are out of your depth if you have to deal with further questions on the subject.

Have you spoken to any people in business about their work? Have you visited any businesses?

Comment: Talk about people who work in business and what they have told you, and why you have found what they said interesting or motivating. When discussing a business that you have visited, give a different example from the one that you talked about in relation to your work experience. Mention what you learned about the workings of this business and how it operates.

Other possible questions

Below are a selection of questions that have been asked in university interviews. You can use these as a basis for a mock interview. Ask someone who does not know you very well to ask you a selection of relevant questions from the list, and then ask them to assess how convincing your answers are. If there are areas that are obviously in need of work, then you can research in preparation for the real interview. However, do not try to learn 'right' answers to all of these questions and then recite them parrot fashion at the interview. If you do this you will come across as having obviously prepared your answers. There is also a danger that you will try to twist a question to suit one of your prepared answers, and you will appear evasive to the interviewer.

- What areas of business are you interested in?
- How does economics affect your daily life?
- What makes a good businessperson or manager?
- Can you give me a quick summary of the underlying reasons for the credit crunch?
- Why do businesses fail?
- What is meant by 'marketing'?
- Why do share prices fluctuate?
- Is it a good thing that the Bank of England sets interest rates in the UK?
- What is microeconomics?
- What is macroeconomics?
- What is globalisation?
- Is globalisation a good thing?
- Who has responsibility for reducing global warming? Businesses or governments?
- Has the Trump campaign in America shown globalisation is going out of fashion in the United States?
- Is the Chinese model of capitalism discredited?
- What will be the impact of Brexit upon global trade?
- Is there likely to be another global economic crisis?
- What is the most significant issue, other than Brexit, facing UK business interests?

- Convince me you should have a place to study here.
- How will the relaxation of the tethering of the Chinese yuan to the US dollar affect this country's economy?
- What will happen if youth unemployment in the EU rises as high as one in six young people by 2020 as predicted?
- What is the difference between a U-shaped and a V-shaped recession?
- Tell me about a difficult situation in the past five years that you dealt with badly and explain how you could have handled it better.
- What achievements in the last five years are you most proud of?
- What are your strengths? Give some examples.
- What are your weaknesses? How do you plan to overcome them?
- Why is the course suitable for you?
- I see you have read X recently. Can you summarise the main arguments?

Current issues in the world of business and economics

Should you be called for interview, the interviewer will probably be looking for a proven interest in and knowledge of current economic issues and/or business case studies. You should already be watching the news and reading relevant publications and newspapers, but you will need to do some extra preparation before you attend an interview. This section is designed to give you an idea of the types of issues that may come up at interview. You will need to do some additional preparation yourself to make sure you are up to date with what has been happening since this guide was published.

Brexit

At the time of writing, Brexit and the UK's future relationship with the European Union after March 2019 is the dominant issue in business and economics in the UK, as despite months of Westminster wrangling nothing had been decided.

The 2002 words of President George W. Bush Secretary of Defense, Donald Rumsfeld, are worth quoting in full because they sum up the current situation very well: '*Reports that say that something hasn't happened are always interesting to me, because as we know, there are known knowns; there are things we know we know. We also know there are known unknowns; that is to say we know there are some things we do not know. But there are also unknown unknowns — the ones we don't know we don't know. And if one looks throughout the history of our country and other free countries, it is the latter category that tend to be the difficult ones.*'

What does this mean for potential students of economics and business studies, as well as for the business leaders and managers of the future? Well, it means that you cannot ignore this issue; it's not going away. Contingency plans for a range of eventualities are needed, and you will need to be well informed of the most recent developments. You will need to be able to offer evidence to support your reasoned judgements. If you get an interview question on Brexit, that you consider impossible to answer due to the uncertainty that surrounds this subject, then you could most definitely take the opportunity to turn the question back to the interviewer.

Other issues

There are other issues that may be more significant in the long run; you could look at these from a business management viewpoint or from a more theoretical economics approach.

- **Climate change.** In late 2018 the UN COP24 summit took place in Poland; the summit was designed to find a way to help the world implement the 2015 Paris Accord. What was decided? What are the main challenges ahead? What is Poland's story with coal mining? What are scientists saying about the Antarctic Ice Sheet? And Arctic sea ice? What do the economic models predict? What are the challenges and opportunities for business?

- **Solar energy.** The growth of this sector is of great interest, particularly because of the role played by competition in energy markets and some new and unusual business models that are arising. How is the City of London hoping to reach its target of 100% renewable energy? What is Robin Hood Energy? What does the company Solar Century do globally? What is the European Bank for Reconstruction and Development doing to promote solar energy?

- **Protectionism.** This is a wider issue than that simply concerning the UK and the EU. There is a suggestion that we are entering an era of de-globalisation, in which the economic gains of globalisation are being rolled back. Protectionism is closely related to nationalism in the political sense, and you may be well advised to watch what is happening in countries such as Brazil, as well as the UK and USA. What is the latest news about tariffs between the USA and China? What is the role of the World Trade Organisation (WTO), and what sanctions can they apply on countries that break their rules?

- **Football.** The global appeal of football as a sport and the power of the big club's brands is an interesting area of study for both business and economics students. Everything we say about protectionism and nationalism is contradicted by sport.

- **Pensions and ageing populations.** In the introduction to this volume it was mentioned that many of you may have to work until you are 70. Pensions are an aspect of the financial sector that is very important, but difficult for young people to take seriously! Management of pension funds is a growth area, as are all the different insurance possibilities surrounding medical care and practical help for the frail and elderly. This will have an impact on taxation and property markets too, and is as much a concern in India and China as it is in Europe and Japan.

For further examples of business case histories, see the latest edition of *The Times 100 Business Case Studies* online at www.business casestudies.co.uk.

After the interview

For Oxford and Cambridge you may have to wait a while before you know how you did. It is often very difficult to judge how it went, and when you review your performance it is natural to focus on what went badly and anything a little silly that you may have inadvertently stated. Please don't worry. It is a fantastic achievement even to get an interview and it is also true that if you fail at one interview you will do better on another occasion. If you fail then do ask for feedback so that you can improve for the future.

Of course, you are also getting to know the institution that is interviewing you. If you hated the interview then maybe you wouldn't enjoy being a student there. Never be afraid to reject them! As the English novelist Kinn Hamilton (aka Catherine Aird) once said: 'If you can't be a good example; then you will have to be a horrible warning.'

TIP!

If you ever feel that you are being bullied and/or made to feel uncomfortable in an interview then you must speak out. That sort of behaviour is unacceptable. Of course you must be polite and respectful too.

---

7 | Non-standard applications

Not everyone applying for a place at a UK university is a sixth-form student studying for A levels; although these students certainly make up the majority of UCAS applicants. In recent years there has been something of a shift. There are a wide variety of qualifications that may make you eligible for a degree course and an increasing number of students may wait some years before applying, may choose to study part-time or may opt for a Foundation degree or Foundation year (see Chapter 1). There are also the international students who recognise the global value of a UK degree; especially in economics and business-related subjects.

The universities themselves have a lot of relevant material available on their websites, as does UCAS. Although the Open University (OU) is not addressed in this volume, they are the specialists in educating mature and part-time students. Applicants to the OU do not apply through UCAS but directly to the OU itself; visit www.open.ac.uk for more information.

We will look at two of the more common types of non-standard application in detail: mature students and international students applying from their own countries.

Mature students

If you are over 21 when you start your course you are classified as 'mature'. About 40% of mature students are over 30 and have family and other commitments.

Mature students fall into three categories.

1. Those with appropriate qualifications – for example, A levels – but who did not go to university and are now applying after a gap of a few years.
2. Those applying for a second degree, having graduated in a different discipline.
3. Those who have no A levels or equivalent qualifications.

Mature students, intending to follow a full-time course, apply to university through UCAS, in much the same way as those at school or college do. If you wish to study a part-time course or distance learning then you apply directly to the degree provider, such as the Open University. The provider themselves will then inform you on the application process.

The entrance requirements for mature students may be different than for sixth-formers. You may have a range of different qualifications and work experience that the admissions tutors will take into account. The prospectus will make it clear how to approach this and if you are in doubt please contact the university directly. There are also access courses that you could take to make up for a lack of formal qualifications; your local college may well offer access to higher education courses. The university sector is keen to widen access and to be more inclusive.

Some business and economics degree courses will ask you to sit an entrance examination especially to test your competency in written English and in mathematics. UCAS has a list of all admissions tests (www.ucas.com/undergraduate/applying-university/admissions-tests) and the individual university prospectus will offer further information, including how and where you sit the tests. Universities may also invite you for interview.

Universities often prefer mature students because they can prove to be more committed to their studies and less interested in the social life than their younger colleagues. If you have already travelled and had experience of workplace environments then you may be more appreciative of the opportunities available, and may also be able to offer a practical contribution to seminar and tutorial groups.

Please refer to Chapter 4 for advice on filling in the UCAS form and selecting a referee.

Mature students are entitled to student finance the same as school leavers are. That is, unless they already have a degree. There may also be additional funding available to help with childcare costs or if you have other dependents. See Chapter 9 for details of the regional student finance bodies, and also check funding options with the university. If you are resident in Scotland these grants are currently more generous than for mature students elsewhere in the UK.

For further information, visit www.ucas.com/undergraduate/student-life/mature-undergraduate-students.

International students

Studying in a country other than your home country is very exciting and may lead to many opportunities for you in the future. If this is something that interests you, the website www.topuniversities.com is a good place to start.

International students fall into three categories.

1. Those who are following A level (or equivalent) programmes either in the UK or in their home countries.
2. Those who are studying for local qualifications that are recognised as being equivalent to A levels in their own countries.
3. Those whose current academic programmes are not equivalent to A levels.

The most recent figures available show, that in 2016/17, there were 2.32 million students studying at higher education institutions in the UK. Of these, about 13% were international students from non-EU countries and 6% from the EU. If you are interested in learning more please look at the website www.universitiesuk.ac.uk.

Individual universities will have greater or lesser proportions of these totals. Tim Bradshaw, chief executive of the Russell Group of universities, said in 2018 that almost a third of their students were from overseas, although he did not state how many of these were postgraduate students. There has been a lot of discussion about international students in the UK media in recent years. The universities themselves value the global range of talent that they can attract; but since 2010 the Home Office has made the visa application process more complex, and there is anxiety about the status of EU students after the UK's planned exit from the European Union in March 2019. One of the main problems is that the UK government includes international students in its immigration targets; despite pressure for this to change, at the time of writing this is still the case. Individual universities have specialists in their administrative staff to help you if you have questions. I would recommend that you contact the university directly because the situation is currently very fluid and uncertain.

Despite these worries, UK universities offer world-class education in economics and business-related subjects. A study published in July 2018 by researchers at University College London shows that overall numbers of international students have increased by 3% in recent years despite the UK dropping from being the second most popular destination for international students after the USA, to third place, with Australia overtaking the UK.

There has also been a growth in what is termed 'Transnational Education' (TNE) with UK universities currently offering their degree programmes in 224 other countries around the world. If you are interested in these courses please check the individual universities' websites for details of what they can offer and where.

Most international students apply through UCAS in the same way as 'Home' students (see Chapter 4). The UCAS website itself offers a lot of guidance for international students, including advice on the equivalence of non-UK qualifications, as do the individual universities' prospectuses. International students may be asked to take entrance examinations by their chosen universities to prove their competency in English and mathematics, and there are also language tests that accompany the visa application process. UCAS has a list of colleges and universities that will offer entrance examinations for business-related degree courses to those with non-standard qualifications.

The UK government has an agency called NARIC (UK National Recognition Information Centre) that deals with all applications to work and study in the UK. The website, www.naric.org.uk/naric, explains how you can get a Certificate of Comparability for any overseas qualifications and also how to apply for the English Language Assessment that may be required by your visa.

If you do not qualify for a Certificate of Comparability it may still be possible for you to apply for a Foundation year or a Foundation degree (see Chapter 1). A very useful source of information is the British Council website: https://study-uk.britishcouncil.org. This tells you exactly what you need to do to study in the UK according to where in the world you are from. It also offers advice to UK residents wishing to study abroad or find overseas work placements.

Applicants to UK universities from EU countries currently face no immigration restrictions and pay the same fees as 'Home' students. This will not change for students starting degree courses in 2019 or 2020 but the position after this has not yet been agreed, and will be subject to the details of a final Brexit withdrawal agreement. The UK Council for International Student Affairs updates its advice regularly: www.ukcisa.org.uk.

UK students applying to study abroad

Many business and economics courses do offer the opportunity to study abroad as part of the degree.

The Erasmus Programme – www.erasmusprogramme.com – was set up in 1987 to encourage student exchange within EU countries. Students study in participating universities usually for three to twelve months and are given financial support. At the time of writing there is no information about what will happen to this after the UK leaves the European Union, but the website gives an overview of what is currently available.

Some high-flying UK students may also be interested in studying in the USA at establishments such as Harvard. If this is of interest to you the website www.savethestudent.org/study-abroad/america/studying-abroad-american-universities.html is very helpful. There is no central system for applications equivalent to UCAS in the USA, and the individual universities have different requirements. You may be asked to submit essays and to take SATs (Standardised Assessment Tests) as part of your application. There are centres in the UK where you can take SATs and there is a fee.

SEND students

SEND stands for Special Educational Needs and Disabilities. If you fall into this category of student your school SEND Coordinating Officer will have a lot of information to help you and the website www. disabilityrightsuk.org is also useful. Different universities offer different levels of support and you will need to check individual websites for details. Many have a team of volunteers who will attend lectures with you and take notes, scribe for exams and help you where necessary. Universities want to be more inclusive and they are building expertise in these areas; there is also a code of practice for the education, health and care of all those with SEND under the age of 25, with the latest guidance published in 2014.

The UCAS application itself has a section where you can disclose any SEND requirements. While you do not have to disclose this information at the outset if you believe it may prejudice your application, please note that an institution cannot discriminate against you based on your disability. UCAS suggest that you contact the individual universities directly and make detailed enquiries as to the facilities that are available for you *before* selecting an institution as one of your five choices. UCAS recommends asking the following questions (to be tailored depending on the nature of your disability).

- Are all the buildings I need to use physically accessible?
- Are there any particular facilities for disabled students?
- Are there any current students with a similar impairment?
- What support do they receive?
- Who will help organise my support?
- Can you help me apply for additional funding if needed?
- Are the methods of teaching and assessment appropriate to my needs?
- What would happen if I started the course and experienced a problem?

There is also additional financial support available for SEND students apart from the standard student finance. This varies according to where you live in the UK, and there are considerations such as the roll out of Universal Credit that you may need to take into account. There are also PIP (Personal Independence Payments) and a DSA (Disabled Students Allowance). Disability Rights UK produce helpful fact sheets for students on their website (www.disabilityrightsuk.org/how-we-can-help/individuals/education/frequently-asked-questions-students).

Extenuating circumstances

Unfortunately not everyone has an easy route through studying for examinations, and things can go wrong during the examination period itself. There is a lot of uncertainty among students about what may happen in these circumstances. Your school examination officer and tutor is the first port of call in this instance. They will know what the examination boards will need to know and you will be asked to provide substantial evidence to support your claim for extenuating circumstances. If it is a medical need then you will have to ask your doctor for a certificate, and they may charge a fee for this service. The examiner who marks your script is not informed of these circumstances; any adjustment to grades is made later by the examination board. The board will want to see evidence of your prior attainment, such as your mock exam papers, to help them with any adjustment, as well as any medical evidence. It is not automatic that they will grant the application for special circumstances; however, they will want to support an applicant in genuine need.

In extenuating circumstances your school may also contact your universities on your behalf, but they do not always welcome such approaches. Universities prefer to deal directly with UCAS. Schools may also contact UCAS or your universities if they have reason to change their predicted grades after the application has been submitted.

8 | Results day

This is a date that will have been in your diary all year, so make sure that you know where you will be on it. You may need to act fast on results day to secure accommodation or negotiate with universities. It is advisable to be in the UK on results day so that you can spend time in school or college if necessary. If this is impossible, you may be able to nominate someone else to collect results on your behalf; your school or college will tell you what to do. However, note that university departments prefer not to speak to your parents/guardians or friends, so ensure that you have good lines of communication wherever you are.

Different examinations publish their results at different times, but A level results have been traditionally published on the third Thursday in August. Scottish Higher results come out in early August, and International Baccalaureate results are issued in July. Your school or college and the universities receive your results the day before results day although they are not allowed to share this information with you. Many schools will have checked your results against your offers and will call you early the next morning if there is a problem. UCAS will also confirm conditional places from midnight so you will know if you got into your choice of university even if you don't know your A level grades. Some qualifications may not be automatically reported to UCAS and the universities, so you may need to send your results to them yourself; in this scenario your chosen university will email you with instructions.

In unusual cases there may be a problem with your results. There may have been an error somewhere in the system and you may have an 'X' rather than a grade on your examination results slip. Your school should already be on top of trying to find the reason for this. In these circumstances the school examinations officer will help you to contact the university to ask them to wait before rejecting you.

Firm choice

If your firm choice is confirmed by UCAS then you can start your celebrations. The university will confirm the place by email and tell you what to do to secure accommodation, etc. UCAS should have already told your insurance choice that you will not be requiring the place, but you can use UCAS Track to confirm all of the above.

Insurance choice

If you have not made the grades for your firm choice but have made the grades for your insurance choice then your insurance choice is automatically confirmed. You made a commitment when you accepted the place, so if you have changed your mind then you may find it difficult to break the contract. You must contact the university yourself to see if they will allow this.

> **TIP!**
>
> Sometimes either your firm choice, your insurance choice or both may make you an offer that is different from the course you originally applied for. In this case, you can choose if you want to take the place or not.

Clearing

If you are rejected by both of your choices because you have not met their grades then you will be automatically entered for Clearing. You will see this on UCAS Track. You can also apply through Clearing if you have not yet submitted an application through UCAS, but you will need to now submit an application to do this; Clearing opens in July for students in this category.

Clearing can be very daunting and your school is likely to have a team of teachers in place to support you through this. The most attractive courses fill very quickly so you may need to start searching very early in the morning. If you almost, but not quite, meet the requirements; it may still be worth making a phone call. You can only make one Clearing choice and you confirm this at first directly with the university. Universities have teams of people answering telephone calls about Clearing places.

If you end up using Clearing, please don't be dismayed. Lots of people end up being very happy with their Clearing choices; often they have adjusted their thinking a little since they made their application six months earlier and may have different priorities as a consequence. You can make this into a positive.

Extra

UCAS Extra is the opportunity to make an extra application through UCAS if your five choices all resulted in rejection. You would have already made your UCAS Extra choice prior to results day. You can use UCAS Track on results day to find out if your Extra choice has been confirmed or rejected. If rejected, you can also apply through Clearing.

Enquiries about results

Enquiries about results – also known as re-marks – occur when students with disappointing results, and after consultation with subject staff, may ask for one or more examination paper to be reviewed by the examination board. It is possible that errors have been made given the pressure with the examination system, but your subject teacher is best

The UK government is concerned that students apply for re-marks in an attempt to 'game' the system. As a consequence of this concern, the rules that the examination boards must follow when dealing with enquiries about results have changed and any mark changes have to be fully justified and scrutinised.

placed to advise on a course of action. You will also know if you made a mistake yourself on the actual exam or if you feel that you did not do your best. Universities will need informing if you intend to do this and they may hold your place open until the end of August. However, universities are not obliged to hold your place for you.

Adjustment

If you have exceeded all expectations and done really well at A level you have the opportunity to 'trade up' from your firm choice. If you are eligible to do this then it will automatically appear on UCAS Track. You will have a short time to consider this option and your favoured universities may not have spaces on courses you wish to take. However, if you are interested in looking for an alternative university place you will not lose your firm choice while you investigate. In this scenario you could also consider withdrawing and reapplying for the following year; but think about the reasons why you made your existing firm choice initially, as it may not be available again in the future.

Reapplying or resitting

Every year there are students who, for a variety of reasons, decide to resit their A levels, and/or reapply to university.

Reapply

Reapplying without resitting has the obvious benefit of knowing your A level results when you apply. This means you can receive unconditional offers and much of the anxiety is taken out of the process.

Before you opt to do this, check if your school or college would be willing to support your new application if you were not a current student, as otherwise you will have to apply as an individual. Also check that universities who may have rejected your previous application are open to reapplicants.

Resit

Resitting can be difficult, especially if specifications have changed, as you may find that you have a completely different course to learn. In the past it was possible to simply resit units that you performed badly in, but these days, with the linear A levels, you will have to resit every paper.

There are specialist colleges, such as MPW, that cater for students who want to resit A levels, or you could choose to manage without extra tuition and resit the exams as an external candidate. The various examination boards offer advice on how you could do this.

While some universities may prefer students who do well at the first attempt, the personal statement is your opportunity to convince them to consider you. However, it is also worth checking that the university won't reject your application on the grounds of resits before it reaches the personal statement phase of consideration.

You may wish to update and amend the personal statement, but there is no obligation to completely revise your personal statement. It would be beneficial to include any relevant additional work experience you have undertaken during this year. However, if you completely reconstruct a personal statement that secured five offers the previous year, you may risk damaging your future chances. Perhaps spend your time more usefully elsewhere, for instance, researching courses and universities.

9 | Fees and funding

There is a significant financial cost to a degree course and most students graduate with a not insignificant debt. The original intent behind tuition fees was that universities would compete by offering different prices for their courses. However, this has not yet come to pass, and most UK students face a £9,250 fee for each year of their course. In 2019 a government review into fees is expected to be published, and there is some thought that degree courses for some subjects will become cheaper while others may become more expensive. You must certainly be alert to any potential changes.

Unfortunately, not every degree at every university will increase potential lifetime earnings by a significant amount. But you will be pleased to know that a degree in economics or business, especially from a highly ranked institution, *does* offer value for money!

Fees

University fees vary according to where your home is in the UK. This has changed a lot recently, but simply, if your home is in England then you will pay more, wherever you study, than students from Wales, Scotland or Northern Ireland. The cost difference is not as great as it was, but you will need to contact the student finance body in your home nation for details. The amount of the student fee loan will be adjusted to account for the differences.

England

Students living in England are required to pay a maximum of £9,250 per year if they are studying in England, Scotland or Northern Ireland, and up to £9,000 if they are studying in Wales.

Wales

Students from Wales pay up to £9,000 if they study in Wales, or up to £9,250 if they study in England, Scotland or Northern Ireland.

Scotland

Students from Scotland who study at Scottish universities are not required to pay tuition fees. They will have to pay fees of up to £9,250 if they study in England or Northern Ireland, and up to £9,000 if they study in Wales.

Northern Ireland

Students living in Northern Ireland will pay up to £4,160 if they attend a university in Northern Ireland, up to £9,250 if they study in England or Scotland, and up to £9,000 if they study in Wales.

International students

EU students currently pay up to £9,250 per year to study at universities in England, £9,000 in Wales, and £4,160 if they study in Northern Ireland. Scottish universities do not currently charge tuition fees for EU students. Currently, EU students are still classed as 'Home' students and EU students starting their course in September 2019 will pay home fees for the duration of their course and remain eligible to apply for funding under the current terms. Following the UK's decision in 2016 to leave the EU, fees for EU students studying at UK institutions beyond 2019 entry are to be negotiated as part of formal withdrawal discussions with the EU.

International students pay a price for their course as decided by their chosen institution and the fees vary considerably. They can pay as little as £10,000 per year or as much as £38,000 per year depending on how popular the course is. If you are British but have been living abroad you may find that you do not qualify for 'Home' student status until you have lived back in the UK for a number of years. The website www.top universities.com/student-info/student-finance/how-much-does-it-cost-study-uk enables comparisons to be made between costs in the UK and elsewhere.

Student loans

You may be eligible to borrow money to pay your tuition fees and also to help with living costs.

The application has some elements that are based on your parents' incomes, so they will have to be involved in the process if you are aged under 25. If you have difficult family circumstances, you can apply to be an estranged student. If you are over 25 you apply in your own right.

You will be charged interest on your student loan from the day you take it out, but do not have to start repaying the loan until you earn over a certain amount; currently £25,000 per annum for students in England and Wales, and £18,330 for students in Scotland and Northern Ireland. The interest rate you will be charged until you start repaying is RPI (Retail Price Index) plus 3%; after you start repaying the interest will be RPI plus a variable rate dependent on your income up to 3%, unless you are earning more than £45,000, in which case it is RPI plus 3%. The RPI is a measure of the rate of inflation. It is less commonly used than the standard CPI (Consumer Price Index) and is usually higher than CPI. At the time of writing RPI is 3.3% so you will be paying 6.3% interest on your student loan. The interest rate will change over time. The best way to find up-to-date information is to go directly to the Student Loans Company (www.slc.co.uk) which administers all student loans on behalf of the government. Your loan will not be kept by them indefinitely; the SLC sells loans to other finance companies and this may impact how you repay the loan in the future. You are advised to look closely into both the advantages and the disadvantages of the system as well as taking a serious look at any possible alternatives. A good place to start is the MoneySavingExpert.com website: www.moneysavingexpert.com/students/student-loans-tuition-fees-changes.

Maintenance loans and grants

There are also maintenance loans available and some students from low-income households may be eligible for grants. The amount of loan will depend upon where you choose to study; for example, London students may be able to access higher loans to compensate for the higher cost of living in the capital.

England

There are maintenance loans of up to £11,354 per year available for students living in England. Further details can be found at www.gov.uk/student-finance and www.hefce.ac.uk.

Wales

For 2019 entry Student Finance Wales (www.studentfinancewales.co.uk) provides Welsh students with a fee grant and a fee loan totalling either £7,650 or £9,000 or £11,250 depending on where you are living. Learning and special support grants are also available.

Scotland

Bursaries and loans of up to £7,625 a year are available from the Student Awards Agency for Scotland (www.saas.gov.uk).

Northern Ireland

Student Finance NI (www.studentfinanceni.co.uk) provides loans up to £6,780. Maintenance and special support grants are also available.

Everything discussed so far applies to full-time students. Of course, there is always the option of part-time and distance learning if you are worried about costs and want to stay in employment.

Scholarships and bursaries

All universities offer fee reductions or help with maintenance living costs to promising students. The details will be on their websites and you will probably need to apply directly to the university for this funding. They may also offer hardship support if you are struggling financially while at university. There is more support around than many people realise and much of this is linked to universities' desire to promote inclusion. The website www.thecompleteuniversityguide.co.uk/university-tuition-fees/other-financial-support/university-bursaries-and-scholarships has a lot of information about where to start looking.

You may also find that there are funds available through local charities in your home town. Check your local library for information.

Sponsorship

Some employers will pay, either fully or in part, for a student to study at university. Most of these schemes have become the new degree apprenticeship schemes discussed in Chapter 1, but if you are already in work you may also find sponsorship. For example, there are cases of students being offered professional contracts with sports teams while also being entered to study part-time for a degree at a university close to the team's location as part of their contracts. This is a way of keeping your options open if you fail to make the grade in your chosen sport or career.

International students

UK authorities require proof that international students can support themselves while they are studying at UK institutions; and international students are also restricted as to any employment opportunities they are able to take. There may also be additional costs, such as healthcare insurance.

Home governments or employers may offer support for studying in the UK.

10| Career paths

Getting into work

High Fliers Research conducted a study of the UK's 100 top employers and found that leading employers were expecting to increase their graduate recruitment by 9.1% in 2019. The biggest growth in vacancies was expected to come from public sector employers, accountancy firms, professional services and engineering and industrial companies, which together intended to recruit more than 1,500 extra graduates in 2019.

Even though the total number of vacancies was set to increase in 2019, over a third of these top recruiters confirmed that applicants without work experience stood little chance of success (see Chapter 2).

Academic background

Many graduates pursuing a business or financial career have degrees in the subject, but not all fall into this category. Some have studied another subject, such as statistics, psychology or English, and join a company on its graduate management-training programme. Others have completed vocational courses. It is also possible to become a successful businessperson by working your way up through the ranks from the shop floor – but this is much less common today than it was in the past.

A degree, even a very good one, is not enough to get on to a prestigious training scheme with a notable company. Graduate recruiters are not usually bothered about your particular degree subject – but they will often want their management trainees to be numerate. Subjects such as marketing, mathematics or statistics, economics, finance or business studies can give you an edge, but some employers still prefer the traditional academic subjects, such as history or classics, even for marketing consumer products. However, there are no degree subjects that completely preclude a graduate from entry on to a management-training scheme. Because managers and economists work in so many different businesses and organisations, and their roles vary from organisation to organisation, there is no single route to a career in these fields. However, you will need certain skills and talents, and a strong academic background helps.

Case study

'The competition to get on to the scheme was intense and we all really had to jump through hoops to secure our places. This started with a fairly straightforward one-to-one interview with the graduate recruitment manager on my university campus. I had prepared well for the interview and had done my research on the company, including looking at its website, and I think this really helped – it certainly gave me confidence. I'd also had a mock interview at my careers service, which was extremely useful. The next stage was an all-day event at the employer's premises. I was with about eight other candidates and we went through a combination of individual interviews with more senior staff and some group exercises, where they gave us a hypothetical problem and asked us to discuss it as a group and come up with some recommendations. I guess it didn't matter too much what our ideas were as long as they made some sense, but I think what they were really looking for was to see how we interacted with each other. That included how we communicated our ideas and also how we listened to others and took their ideas on board. We were also given a 30-minute numeracy test where we were not allowed to use a calculator – so remember to brush up on your tables! I must have passed all those tests, as I was then offered a place on the scheme to start the following September.'

Graham, mathematics and management graduate,
now a graduate trainee

Skills and qualities

If you have a good academic background, it will be your personal qualities that will often win you the job. Most companies' recruitment brochures will give you a fairly comprehensive list of skills and qualities they are looking for, and may include:

- communication skills (these are paramount)
- the ability to think logically and clearly and to analyse accurately
- the ability to research facts and to be able to assess what information is important
- absorption: assessment of the importance of lots of very detailed information and seeing its implications
- organisational ability
- the ability to work with anyone at any level and get the best out of them
- building and maintaining working relationships, and summing up people accurately

- the ability to co-operate and contribute to a team
- numeracy
- self-confidence
- sound business awareness
- natural authority and leadership
- the ability to think strategically, see the whole picture and conceptualise
- the ability to keep targets in focus and make sure they are reached
- the ability to motivate others, recognise their potential and delegate responsibility
- high ethical standards
- the ability to prioritise information and tasks.

Career opportunities

Business and management graduates

Graduates in business and management enter a very wide range of careers. These include accountancy, investment banking, insurance, management consultancy, information technology, marketing, business journalism, the media and the legal profession – to name but a few. The list of options is almost endless, but it must be highlighted that many of the careers, and the employers recruiting such graduates, are increasingly global.

How often do you hear someone say 'I'd like to work in business' or 'I'd like to be a manager'? These are not uncommon career aims, but more often than not people do not have a real understanding of what being a businessperson or manager actually involves. The terms are sometimes used as meaning 'being successful' rather than anything to do with the concept of the work. So, first things first: if you are thinking about a career in business or management, you need to find out what management means and what the typical functions or departments in businesses are.

Whenever you open a newspaper and look at the jobs section, every second advertisement has the word 'manager' in its title. Is this just a ploy to attract applicants or is it that some form of management is integral to many jobs? And if so, what do all these people do? Well, they all do different things, and work for an enormous variety of organisations. Yet at the same time they all have certain responsibilities and tasks in common.

The most straightforward definition of management in business terms could be 'the achievement of objectives through other people'. So, the primary difference between managerial and other types of work is that it involves getting other people to do the necessary work rather than doing all the tasks yourself.

Essentially, anyone who manages is responsible – and accountable – for making sure that whatever department or project they are in charge of runs smoothly and successfully. (Depending on the type of employer, this usually means profitably too!) Now this obviously means that you bask in the glory – and, with luck, the profits – when all goes well. But when things go wrong, as they inevitably do at times, the manager is the person who will be taken to task because it is he or she who is ultimately responsible for what happens. So you can draw the following conclusions about the role of management in business.

- Every job has some managerial aspects. Even the most junior clerical workers must ensure that others co-operate with them so that they can do their job.
- No job is exclusively managerial. Everyone has to perform some tasks for themselves.
- Management is not just about status or being paid better. Some professionals and other specialists with no real management responsibilities are often more senior and have a higher salary than many managers.
- The term management also covers a vast range of other activities, including supervision, organisation, administration and leadership. (The job title 'executive' is sometimes used in the same context as 'manager'.)

Management is undoubtedly a skill in its own right and is essentially the same in whatever field it is carried out. Good managers are not confined to managing work that they are capable of doing themselves. Indeed, in the higher levels of management, it can be an advantage not to have the bias that specialist knowledge can bring.

Economics graduates

Many economics graduates follow business or management careers. Economics degrees provide graduates with a range of analytical skills, and an in-depth knowledge of how domestic and global money markets operate. In particular, businesses that operate on a global scale are keen to recruit economists. There are many other opportunities open to economics graduates. Economists are employed by banks and other financial institutions, public bodies, political parties, governments, non-governmental organisations and universities. Newspapers often survey the UK's top companies or biggest employers, and the majority of these will employ economists. Some will be banks, accountancy firms or management consultants, but government bodies such as the NHS also recruit economists. The government's own economics service employs over 1,400 economists. Good economists are able to analyse information, mostly in numerical form, and draw conclusions from it. They are generally strong mathematicians as well as being able to understand theoretical models and apply them to real-life situations.

Case study

Jenny studied A levels in economics, mathematics and physics at a sixth-form college in London. She found all three subjects worked well together, and she was able to use ideas and techniques from her physics to help her with her economics.

'I found that being able to understand the ideas behind proving theories and equations in A level Physics was very helpful in my economics. In physics, you look at experimental results and then see how they can either prove, disprove or modify an equation or theory. A good example of this is in quantum physics, where one set of experiments seems to prove that light is a wave, whereas another set shows it is a particle – two very different things.

'Economics is the same, but the experiments are on a much larger scale – the global economy, for example! Economists come up with conflicting models to try to explain or predict how economies can develop and change, and we then try to see whether the results of the "experiment" – that is, what is actually happening in the world – support the theories.'

At university, Jenny chose an economics degree course that involved a good deal of mathematical application, as she enjoyed this aspect of the subject. She now works for a large international bank, looking at the impact of changes in commodity prices and how they affect the economy.

Beginning your career

A number of large companies have graduate training schemes for new graduates. With such companies, training is usually undertaken in-house through formal programmes and on-the-job experience, and is sometimes combined with study for a professional qualification.

However, lots of graduates start their careers in small organisations that may not have any formal training programme. Although this is less structured, it is possible to get a wealth of early experience and responsibility by being thrown in at the deep end, while gaining an excellent overview of how the whole organisation operates.

There is no right or wrong answer when it comes to whether you join a big or small organisation initially. You should consider how much structure and formal training you want and look for an organisation that will give you this. If a firm belongs to the government initiative Investors in People, it will place great emphasis on training and career development. Traditionally, people reach a management position after a number of years of experience in a specialist function, such as sales, marketing, personnel or finance.

Many firms have moved away from the traditional hierarchical structure based on business functions (such as production, marketing, etc.) to one based on project teams. Working in a smaller team like this can be very exciting because there is often a greater sense of urgency and camaraderie among the various members. You need to learn how to reach decisions in a group and realise that everyone is different, but that this does not mean they do not have important skills to contribute. You also learn that no one is perfect and everyone can make mistakes – including you!

Information technology (IT) really has changed the way we are able to work. Some firms now even consist of 'virtual teams', i.e. people who work together but do not share an office. They may be scattered geographically and communicate via their mobile phones and the internet. They may even work for that company on only a few days every week, doing something else for the rest of their time.

One consideration is to delay the beginning of your career by studying for a master's degree, most notably a Master of Business Administration (MBA). There are many MBA courses in the UK. A useful website would be www.find-mba.com/most-popular/uk-ireland, which lists the 50 most popular courses in the UK and Ireland in terms of the number of views each receives. There are many different courses, so you need to establish a similar process to your undergraduate degree to find the right course for you.

There are relative advantages in pursuing a master's degree, but it is not a decision that needs to be taken in the final year of your undergraduate degree. Many graduates enter the job market, identify an area of interest and then search for an appropriate master's degree. Remember, if you enter the world of business and management, you are not limited to an MBA degree. You may wish to discuss your options with an employer, for many companies encourage their employees to further their education. You may be able to secure funding, time release and other forms of support. The key point is to keep your options open and undertake research before any further academic study.

Typical business functions

We will now look at some of the most popular areas of business and management in more detail.

Marketing

The marketing function in business is to make people aware that a product or service exists, and encourage people to buy it. This often requires identifying the most likely groups of buyers and targeting them in specific ways. TV advertising, for example, requires considerable planning and market research. Marketing professionals will have researched the product and its rivals and identified how and where they want to place their product in the market to maximise sales, promote brand loyalty or achieve market penetration, and so on. They will commission an advertising agency to come up with a suitable campaign and monitor how this affects sales. Psychologists are often involved in devising advertising slogans or images that will stick in the mind and that will be recalled or influence us when we see the product.

Careers in marketing are often varied; many people who have worked in marketing later move on to advertising agencies or to work as publicity consultants. Marketing tends to attract people who are creative and good at thinking up original and innovative ideas. However, there are also many jobs in market research that require people who can direct discussion groups, design and conduct surveys and process the statistical evidence. For these jobs, it is important to have good numeracy and communication skills.

Most business studies degrees will include modules on marketing. If you are sure that you want a career in marketing, you could decide to choose a joint honours degree such as business studies with marketing, or a single honours degree in marketing. Some art colleges will also offer specialised marketing degree courses, such as fashion marketing. These tend to involve more creative and practical work than those offered on the more traditional courses.

Case study

'I went to university and studied for a degree in business and management because I wanted to prove to my family that I could be a successful businesswoman. My degree gave me the confidence I needed. I learnt how to do my own accounts, about the importance of tracking all costs and the principles of marketing. Honestly? Not everything I studied was directly useful, but I grew up while I was away and broadened my experience. If I could go back in time I wouldn't change my choice of degree!'

Pippa, business and management graduate

> ## Case study
>
> After graduating with a BA in Business Administration, Joanna decided she wanted to combine her qualification with her love of fashion. She became a marketing assistant at a global company and has worked her way up through the industry.
>
> 'The first job I had was a bit of a shock. Translating what I'd learnt in theory into practice was the biggest challenge and in hindsight this culture shock would have been limited if I'd had some more work experience. I got my head down and learnt as much as I could before deciding to work abroad. I worked as a marketing executive for a global retailer in Sydney. While I enjoyed my role, I found that I was drawn to the more creative aspects of the industry. Upon my return to the UK I took an evening class in fashion journalism at the London College of Fashion and have since moved into fashion copywriting for a major online retailer of designer fashion. My background in business complements this more creative role and I think it enables me to see the bigger picture rather than just the objectives of my own role.'

Sales

Another aspect of business is sales. This work is increasingly paid on commission only. In other words, if you do not sell anything you do not get paid. On the other hand, if you are good at selling, the rewards can be fantastic.

What you sell will depend on the business you work in. Books, advertising, professional services, timeshares, cars, stocks and shares, ideas, computer software – anything that a business produces needs to be sold. The work may involve travelling as a rep or may be desk-based telesales, for example. As a manager you will also be responsible for the sales team, whether it is in-house or made up of reps based around the country or abroad.

You can be taught sales techniques as part of a business studies course, but you need a basic aptitude to sell really effectively. If you have natural selling skills, this might be an area to consider. If you are not sure whether a job in sales is for you, your summer holidays could be a useful testing period. There are lots of jobs where you could try out your sales technique, such as working on a stall in a fair or market and encouraging people to come and buy your products, or doing work experience in an estate agents or car showroom to see how the people working there use their sales techniques to encourage customers to make a purchase.

As well as being an integral part of a business-related degree, there are more specialised degree courses available that focus on this area, such as marketing and sales or sales management.

Case study

Neil has been working at a large retail outlet as a department manager for the past two years. He graduated three years ago with a 2.i degree in Business Studies from Kingston University and successfully got his job by applying through the university milk round. After taking a year off, which combined temporary work with travelling, he joined the company on its 18-month graduate training programme.

'My training has been excellent and I am still learning all the time. I have been on short courses covering topics such as teamwork, negotiating skills, customer service and management skills. I started my training in the soft furnishings department and am now the department manager for the books department. I have been exposed to all aspects of running a department, from working on the shop floor and serving customers to learning about stocktaking and display.

Personnel

Personnel work, or human resources (HR) as it is often called, covers every aspect of a business relating to the people in it. As a personnel officer, you would be involved in the recruitment and training of staff, implementing company policies and government legislation affecting employees and maintaining employee records.

In large companies, HR departments analyse staffing requirements, agree targets and devise selection procedures. They organise staff appraisals and administer training and management development policies, and deal with disciplinary matters as they arise. Personnel departments in some very large organisations will often be split into different functions, such as training and graduate recruitment.

In smaller companies, there might be only one or two people who cover all personnel issues, and these may be a small part of their whole job function. So if you were to join a small administrative department you might get more of an overview of personnel than in quite a large company, where your training might be more specialised. In small companies, it is also quite common for departmental managers to deal with personnel issues such as training and discipline.

Personnel work is often challenging and emotionally demanding. The skills required include objectivity (the ability to see all sides of a problem), a reasonable level of numeracy, organising skills and an understanding of all types of people.

Management degrees are particularly suitable for students who are interested in following this route, because they will include modules on the psychology of dealing with people. There are also legal issues to be taken into consideration – these are also likely to be offered as part of a management-related degree. Most business courses will also provide students with the opportunity to find out more about personnel work and HR, but it is likely to form a smaller part of the course. You might also look at business and personnel or business and HR management courses.

Case study

Ryan graduated with a 2.i degree in Business Studies. He had done an industrial placement with a leading accountancy firm and was accepted on to its very competitive graduate training scheme. Ryan eventually plans to go into HR, but the firm he is working for requires all staff of a certain level to be qualified accountants, so he is currently going through his professional accountancy exams.

'It's tough and to be honest, accountancy does not appeal to me in the long run, but it will give me an understanding of the industry that would be impossible if I went straight into HR. Once I've completed my training, I'll be able to transfer to the HR department of my company and work abroad if I wish. I'll also always have my accountancy qualifications as a back-up.'

Finance

The financial aspects of a business are commonly regarded as the most important. If there is no cash in the tills and the bank wants the overdraft repaid yesterday, that spells trouble. All firms have accounts departments responsible for sending out invoices and chasing debtors, paying suppliers and drawing up the company's annual accounts. This is known as financial accounting and refers to keeping track of the financial side of the business after the transactions have happened. Financial accounting lets the senior management know how well the business has done in the past year. However, it does not prepare for the future.

Planning for the future is called management accounting. With this, firms draw up extensive and detailed budgets for every department so that they can keep a tight control on costs and are therefore less likely to make mistakes in the year ahead. Both types of accounting make extensive use of IT.

Accountancy does not have to be boring or deskbound. It can be a good way to join a creative team in the media industry or film industry – areas that are often difficult to get into otherwise.

The financial sector covers a wide range of careers and employers. These include banks, building societies, insurance companies and accountancy firms. All of these organisations would be open to recruiting graduates with a degree in business or management, as long as their A level grades (or equivalent) are good enough and they have a good degree, which usually means a minimum classification of 2.i.

All the major clearing banks run graduate training schemes that give you the opportunity to train and work in many aspects of the bank's function over a period of around 18 months. This will usually mean moving around the country for your various placements. In the case of the banks, you will normally be encouraged to study for the Chartered Banker Institute professional examinations. Once experienced, you might be promoted to, for example, a branch manager. In this role you could be involved with individuals and corporate clients. As a trainee, you might have a spell in a department marketing corporate services and then move into a role as a personal accounts executive.

In addition to their general graduate training schemes, most of the large banks also recruit graduates directly into their computing departments. This does not necessarily require you to have a computer science degree, and most of these training schemes are open to graduates from any discipline. Most careers in the financial sector will require you to be meticulously accurate and good with figures. You will also need to have good interpersonal skills, excellent IT skills and to be able to work effectively as part of a team.

Business studies, economics and management degrees will all cover aspects of finance and accounting, as these are equally applicable to the running of a small business, a government organisation or a country's economy. A business- or management-related degree will look at the more practical aspects of finance – accounting procedures, financial management, legal issues and banking procedures – whereas an economics degree will look at these issues on a larger scale and in a more mathematical and theoretical way.

There are also more specialised degrees available for those students who have a clear idea of their future direction: accounting, accounting and finance, and banking and finance courses are widely available and very popular.

Purchasing

Most organisations, including manufacturing and insurance companies, as well as public-sector organisations, require expert purchasers or buyers.

'Purchasing' is a term mainly used in industry. 'Buying' tends to be used in retailing, and other organisations will often use the term 'supplies'.

But the principles of the job are the same. Purchasing managers are now part of a wider profession known as supply chain management. Purchasing is probably at its most complicated in the manufacturing industry, where products such as cars are assembled from many different components. The purchasing manager may be involved from the start, when the design engineers begin to specify the raw materials and the parts needed, by pinpointing suppliers and sorting out any problems with new designs.

Skills required for purchasing include the ability to work well with figures, accuracy, and the ability to digest technical and other data quickly and easily, as well as excellent communication skills.

Business and management degrees will cover topics that are relevant to students interested in this area, and are likely to use case histories and current businesses as illustrations. Economics degrees will include courses in microeconomics (which deals with how individuals and businesses manage and plan their finances) and macroeconomics (how countries' economies depend on income and expenditure). These courses will treat purchasing in a more theoretical and mathematical way. You could also investigate purchasing and supply, or business and purchasing degree courses.

Start-ups

The term 'start-up' first emerged in the 1970s, but only became popular at the beginning of the twenty-first century with small companies, usually in the field of technology and digital operations, offering an innovative or niche product with the potential for rapid growth. The initial staff numbers tend to be low, but the vast majority of the staff will provide either highly skilled or very specific skills. One of the key features of start-ups is prompt adaptation to developing market trends with scope for rapid expansion.

Graduates with business and economic degrees may either be involved in founding start-ups or becoming involved at an early stage in the life of a company. The disadvantages of start-ups are fairly clear: long hours and low job security, but there are significant potential advantages beyond the obvious possibility of considerable financial reward if the company has identified and exploited the proverbial 'gap in the market'. Start-up companies offer young graduates the chance to enjoy a measure of autonomy not usually available, or at least immediately available, in larger, more heavily structured companies. Also, you may be interested in business, finance and economic developments, but you do not view yourself as a 'corporate' individual. Start-ups generally offer a more relaxed, less regimented power structure, enabling you to input ideas into the company in a more receptive environment. The website

Startups (https://startups.co.uk) would be a good place to begin. Also, start-up companies might also be more receptive to potential internships or work experience applications if you can offer the company some relevant previous experience or expertise.

Transport management

Some of the world's biggest businesses are involved in the movement of people and goods, and transport managers are responsible for the safety and efficiency of passenger or freight services. This might include managing and administering places such as airports, railway stations, ports and bus or freight depots on a day-to-day basis. Tasks could include scheduling and timetabling. The role of the transport manager also covers the commercial elements open to all businesses, such as finance, marketing and personnel management.

If there is an accident, it is the job of the transport manager to investigate and take any necessary action. A vital task is to ensure that health and safety regulations are enforced. To be successful in transport management you must be good at organising and planning and enjoy working with figures. It is important that you can remain calm under pressure, but are able to think quickly and logically on your feet. Teamwork and good interpersonal skills are essential.

Both business- and management-related degrees would provide the necessary knowledge and skills for a career in transport management. You could also look at more specialised transport management degrees.

Project management

Many firms organise their staff into specific project teams instead of the traditional functions of marketing, finance, personnel and so on. People on a specific project will come from a variety of different business backgrounds and work together for the duration of that project, often as a team, sharing tasks and responsibilities. You could lead the project as project manager, which requires great skill but can also be very exhilarating.

Management degrees would be the most suitable for a student aiming at project management as a future career. There are many specialised degree courses available, including building project management, project engineering and even public art project management.

Management consultancy

The International Guide to Management Consultancy: The Evolution, Practice and Structure defines a management consultant as an independent and qualified person who provides a professional service to business, the public and other undertakings. Management consultants identify and investigate problems in a company concerned with strategy, policy, markets, organisation, procedures and methods. Generally, a team is sent to spend time with the organisation to find out what the problems are. It then comes up with a set of recommendations for action by collecting and analysing the facts, still keeping in mind the broader management and business implications.

Finally, it discusses and agrees on the most appropriate courses of action with the client, and may remain at the company for a short period to help implement these strategies.

Management consultants are high-fliers – they can be recruited from the top graduates, but they are usually people with business experience. This is because, if you are going to have any credibility in advising others how to run their businesses, you need real-life understanding of such issues. You will also need to be quite sensitive and tactful and have a good deal of maturity. Excellent numeracy, teamwork and inter-personal skills are all essential, as is a strong academic background (usually meaning at least a 2.i degree from a prestigious university).

Management degrees would provide a good deal of useful background and training for anyone interested in a management consultancy career. Given the need for analytical and numeracy skills, economics graduates would also satisfy this requirement. There are many very specialised management degrees on offer; you can find these using the 'Course Search' facility on the UCAS website.

General management in large companies

Large companies will often have general managers who are responsible for the general running and operational details of a business. Their role is to liaise with other departments, monitor how members of staff are recruited and make sure that training is kept up to date. The general manager is also responsible for ensuring that profit targets are met, as well as keeping an eye on the marketing and promotional aims of the organisation.

Several large businesses run training schemes for both school-leavers and graduates as management trainees. Most schemes provide an initial period of training, often 12 to 18 months, in which you are placed in a number of departments in the organisation, such as finance, sales and marketing. This is a great opportunity to try out different areas and find out what you like and what you are good at – a bit like a Foundation course. At the end of the training period, you can decide where you want to specialise.

A number of companies have fast-track management programmes with accelerated training and early responsibility. Many university management departments will have close links with large companies to provide internships, training or to arrange sandwich-year placements.

Management in small businesses

Large company management training schemes, especially with blue chip organisations, are always going to be the most competitive to get on to. You will certainly get a good and thoroughly structured training from them, but you should not overlook the often excellent experience you can gain from a smaller organisation.

In a smaller organisation, you will probably be thrown in at the deep end and are unlikely to have very specific responsibilities, but you will see at close hand the prizes and pitfalls of a career in business. You will also see demonstrated the difference effective marketing can make, and gain first-hand experience of things such as dealing with banks and coping with disgruntled customers – in other words, the reality of working in business.

Managing a small business requires practical skills as well as an understanding of theory. Most business degrees will focus on these skills.

Entrepreneurship

If you have a good idea, have some experience of constructing cash-flow forecasts and are not afraid of failure or hard work, setting up your own company could be your route into the world of business. Richard Branson started his business empire while still at school, as did Alan Sugar. Other useful role models might include the entrepreneur James Dyson or Karren Brady (vice-chairman of West Ham United).

However, it is more common for someone to set up on their own after gaining experience in another organisation. If you are thinking of starting your own business, you will need a lot of the skills and business awareness that are best gained from employment. Added to which, you will need to be innovative and creative, energetic and resilient, persistent and prepared to work long hours. You will need to be realistic in your business plans, and able to adapt rapidly to changing circumstances. It can be very fulfilling to be self-employed, but make sure it is for you before choosing this route.

Successful entrepreneurs tend to be dynamic people with a clear vision of what they want to achieve. Degree courses cannot teach students to be successful entrepreneurs, but a degree in business studies will give a budding entrepreneur the practical skills and knowledge base to supplement his or her ambitions and ideas. There are many degree courses that focus on entrepreneurship, often combined with other disciplines such as mathematics or a language.

> ## Case study
>
> While completing his A levels, Nick worked part-time in a high-end jewellery shop. He studied business administration at university and continued working at the jewellers throughout all of his holidays. This gave him an insight into the industry and invaluable contacts which he used to get a work-experience placement at a top auction house in London and later a similar, paid role in New York. Nick now runs his own successful diamond-sourcing business.
>
> 'In my mid-twenties when my peers started to get engaged, I realised that I was in a position to help friends get something very unique. That was when I decided to set up my own, bespoke diamond ring business. My background in business was invaluable and I was able to handle the marketing, branding, accounts and operations alone at first. After the company gathered some momentum I began to outsource some of the activity, which gives me support when I need it without the burden of employing full-time staff.'

What makes a good manager?

Many students are attracted by the thought of a managerial career. It has the advantage of being open to graduates from any discipline and work is rewarded on merit – your worth is judged by your performance. A managerial career does not depend on seniority, and it can offer its own rewards, stemming from practical achievement in a job where results can be measured. While a degree in management will not automatically make you a good manager (just as a business studies degree does not necessarily make you a successful businessperson), it does provide you with the academic and practical skills that are necessary for a successful career in management. Bear in mind, however, that there are other ways to acquire these skills.

Different managerial roles require different skills, but a general idea of what companies require of their managers is given in the next section.

Management skills

Managers today have to work in an ever-changing and complex business environment; they need to use an increasing number of analytical methods and techniques. An important skill lies in knowing which techniques to use in a given situation, and how to use them correctly. Here are the main skills you will need to be an effective manager.

Leadership

Good managers are also leaders. The real challenge of management lies in empowering your team to take charge of a project or goal and together achieve more than they believed they could possibly handle. On a management degree course, you would look at different leadership models.

Delegating

Management involves delegating power and responsibility appropriately, not preventing others from developing by hanging on to everything, but equally not giving colleagues unachievable workloads or putting impossible expectations on them.

Getting things done

Good managers are the people who get things done, and they do this by inspiring and encouraging the people working with them.

Teamwork

Teamwork plays a huge part in successful management and is the main reason why employers frequently ask candidates about their extra-curricular achievements and activities. Playing a sport, taking part in dramatic productions or being involved in a school magazine or university society all show an ability to work in a team.

Managing your own work

It is essential that the good manager is effective at managing their own workload well and setting standards for their team. This means setting an example in areas such as good organisation, timekeeping, commitment, personal presentation and honesty.

Managing stress

Because of the pressures of management, good managers will do whatever they can to avoid the effects of undue stress on their physical and mental health – and therefore their productivity. This means having problem-solving skills: you will need to notice if a stressful situation is developing and affecting a team or its members, and be able to deal with it successfully.

Political awareness

Every organisation has its own culture and politics. Good managers will be aware of the context in which they work, including the sensitivities of other people and other departments, so that they can be most effective at motivating their teams.

Managing functions

The management role is broad-ranging, and responsibilities can be spread over several business areas or functions. For example:

- operations: maintaining and improving delivery of the service or product for which they are responsible
- finance: budgeting and monitoring the use of resources
- people: motivating those they work with
- information: communicating effectively with everyone at all levels.

Languages

Language skills are essential, and already more than half of the world's population speak a second language. To enable effective communication with others, you need to cope with the nuances of speech as well as understanding documents such as letters and reports. If you are an English speaker you can get by in Scandinavia, the Netherlands, Germany, much of Central and Eastern Europe and sometimes in France and Belgium without local language skills. (This would not, perhaps, be so easy in Spain or Italy.) But in any situation, you will always be at an advantage if you are able to hold at least a simple conversation in the language of the country in which you are working.

11 | Further information

Reading

Most universities include some selected sources on a reading list for their potential undergraduates. There are, of course, dozens of books you could choose to read or to dip into. This is just a selection collated from suggestions provided by ex-students, current students and fellow economics teachers for their thoughts. Some of these will help you in terms of 'reading around' your A level and some may be worth mentioning on a personal statement. The books may also help you to understand what a degree in these subjects may involve and may also inspire you to follow a particular path post graduation.

Beyond the following list of books, it is assumed that you are reading *The Economist* magazine, the *Financial Times* and other broadsheets regularly; as well as following a diverse range of journalists, economists and business gurus on Twitter. There are also television documentaries and news programmes as well as movies with relevant themes. For example, the scene in the bank in *Mary Poppins* illustrates very effectively what happens when depositors all want to withdraw their cash at the same time. However, if you want to learn, reading is essential. Make sure that you keep a reading diary and jot down useful quotes and references.

- **The 80 minute MBA**, Richard Reeves and John Knell (Headline, 2014). Very accessible and easy to read, with good illustrations; a solid introduction to business management.

- **Elinor Ostrom's Rules for Radicals**, Derek Wall (Pluto Press, 2017). Elinor Ostrom has been, to date, the only woman to have won a Nobel Prize for Economics (in 2009). She takes a different approach to property rights compared to many modern neoliberal economists, and this short volume about her work will be an interesting addition to your knowledge.

- **Freakonomics: A Rogue Economist Explores the Hidden Side of Everything**, Steven D. Levitt and Stephen J. Dubner (Penguin, 2007). This is an oldie; but if you're not much of a reader then it certainly is the book for you. The authors have written other books since this, but almost all students enjoy reading and discussing

Freakonomics. It may also help explain why economics struggles with diversity.

- **GDP: A Brief but Affectionate History**, Diane Coyle (Princeton University Press, 2015). An understanding of economic growth and how we measure the size of an economy is as of much interest to those in business as to economists, and this book is easy to read.

- **The Hard Thing About Hard Things**, Ben Horowitz (Harper Business, 2014). Ben Horowitz is a well-known and well-respected Silicon Valley entrepreneur.

- **The Intelligent Investor**, Benjamin Graham (HarperBusiness, 2003). Originally written in 1949 and said by many to be the best book about markets ever written.

- **International Business: The New Realities**, S. Tamer Cavusgil, Gary A. Knight & John R. Riesenberger (Pearson, 2016). An easy-to-read introduction to globalisation and how businesses can expand internationally.

- **The Logic of Life: The Rational Economics of an Irrational World**, Tim Harford (Random House, 2009). Anything by Tim Harford is worth reading. Tim is known as 'The Undercover Economist' and writes for general interest in the *Financial Times*. He also presents *More or Less* on Radio 4, which is available as a podcast.

- **The New Confessions of an Economic Hit Man**, John Perkins (Ebury Press, 2018). Looks at how developing countries become indebted and some of the less ethical business practices in use around the globe.

- **Poor Economics: A Radical Rethinking of the Way to Fight Global Poverty**, Abhijit Bannerjee and Esther Duflo (Public Affairs, 2012). There are perspectives on economics other than the perspectives of middle-aged white men.

- **Post Capitalism: A Guide to our Future**, Paul Mason (Penguin, 2016). An alternative to more mainstream thinking and provides food for thought.

- **The Rise and Fall of American Growth: The U.S. Standard of Living since the Civil War**, Robert J. Gordon (Princeton University Press, 2017). Reinforces the importance of the USA in the global economy.

- **Social Ecology in the Digital Age**, Daniel Stokols (Academic Press, 2017). Social ecology is an important modern concept and this book claims to help us understand the existential challenges of the 21st century: global climate change and climate-change denial, environmental pollution, biodiversity loss, food insecurity, disease pandemics, inter-ethnic violence and the threat of nuclear war, cyber crime, the Digital Divide, and extreme poverty and income inequality.

- **Unshakeable: Your Guide to Financial Freedom**, Tony Robbins (Simon & Schuster, 2017). The author interviews 50 of the greatest financial minds in the world and looks at how to invest wisely, including through crashes and crises.

- **Who Runs Britain?.... and Who's To Blame for The Economic Mess We're In**, Robert Peston (Hodder, 2008). Explains how the government is not as powerful as it seems because the country is run by the super-rich.

Websites

Throughout this volume useful weblinks have been cited; here they are again in one place and listed chapter by chapter.

Introduction

When researching different universities; look at different survey results to add a range of viewpoints:

- www.timeshighereducation.com/student/news/national-student-survey-2018-overall-satisfaction-results
- https://unistats.ac.uk
- www.whatuni.com/student-awards-winners/university-of-the-year.

Chapter 1

To find out about new approaches to economics, and courses without a big emphasis on mathematics:

- www.rethinkeconomics.org/about/our-story.

If you are interested in studying overseas:

- www.prospects.ac.uk.

Information about professional accreditation:

- www.brightnetwork.co.uk/career-path-guides/accounting-audit-tax/how-to-job-accounting-financial-management/guide-to-accounting-qualifications
- https://careers.icaew.com.

Chapter 2

For programmes to give you experience of future careers and to enhance your application:

- www.ncsyes.co.uk/what-is-ncs
- www.socialmobility.org.uk.

For volunteering:

- www.do-it.org
- www.timebank.org.uk
- http://vinspired.com
- https://volunteeringmatters.org.uk
- www.youthaction.org.uk.

Chapter 3

The first website to check for anything student related in the UK including degree quality:

- www.officeforstudents.org.uk.

For information about employment after university:

- www.graduate-jobs.com.

For advice about A level choices:

- https://russellgroup.ac.uk.

Chapter 4

The first place to seek help with your UCAS (university application) form and to register your application:

- www.ucas.com/students
- www.ucas.com/undergraduate/applying-university/filling-your-ucas-undergraduate-application.

Information to help you prepare for Oxbridge pre-interview assessments:

- www.admissionstesting.org/for-test-takers/cambridge-pre-interview-assessments
- www.admissionstesting.org/for-test-takers/thinking-skills-assessment/tsa-oxford/about-tsa-oxford.

Chapter 7

Studying at the Open University as an alternative to traditional university courses:

- www.open.ac.uk.

If you want to know about studying outside the UK:

- www.topuniversities.com.

If you are an overseas (or UK) student and want to know more about UK universities, this organisation describes itself as the 'collective voice' of the universities, and has lots of facts and figures:

- www.universitiesuk.ac.uk

If you need to check if your qualifications are acceptable to UK universities and employers:

- www.naric.org.uk/naric.

The most useful source of information for any UK student wishing to study abroad or for any overseas student wishing to study in the UK:

- https://study-uk.britishcouncil.org.

For advice on visas and all immigration matters:

- www.ukcisa.org.uk.

For study in Europe:

- www.erasmusprogramme.com/the_erasmus.php.

For study in the USA:

- www.savethestudent.org/study-abroad/america/studying-abroad-american-universities.html.

If you have special educational needs or disabilities:

- www.disabilityrightsuk.org.

Chapter 9

If you want information about the price of a university education:

- www.topuniversities.com/student-info/student-finance/how-much-does-it-cost-study-uk.

For information on student finance:

- www.gov.uk/student-finance
- www.saas.gov.uk
- www.slc.co.uk.
- www.studentfinanceni.co.uk
- www.studentfinancewales.co.uk.

For information on bursaries and scholarships:

- www.thecompleteuniversityguide.co.uk/university-tuition-fees/other-financial-support/university-bursaries-and-scholarships.

Further useful websites

Business and financial news

- www.bbc.co.uk/news
- www.businessweek.com
- www.economist.com
- www.ft.com
- www.telegraph.co.uk/finance

Financial organisations

- www.worldbank.org
- www.wto.org

University entrance

- www.guardian.co.uk/education/universityguide
- www.ucas.com

Useful addresses

ACCA UK
The Adelphi
1–11 John Adam Street
London WC2N 6AU
Tel: 0141 582 2000 (ACCA Connect)
Fax: 020 7059 5050
Email: info@accaglobal.com
www.accaglobal.com

British Chambers of Commerce
65 Petty France
London SW1H 9EU
Tel: 020 7654 5800
www.britishchambers.org.uk

Chartered Institute of Logistics and Transport
Earlstrees Court
Earlstrees Road
Corby NN17 4AX
Tel: 01536 740100
www.ciltuk.org.uk

Chartered Institute of Management Accountants
The Helicon
One South Place
London EC2M 2RB
Tel: 020 8849 2251
www.cimaglobal.com

Chartered Institute of Marketing
Moor Hall
Cookham
Maidenhead SL6 9QH
Tel: 01628 427120
www.cim.co.uk

Chartered Institute of Personnel and Development
151 The Broadway
London SW19 1JQ
Tel: 020 8612 6200
www.cipd.co.uk

Chartered Institute of Purchasing and Supply
Easton House
Church Street
Easton on the Hill
Stamford PE9 3NZ
Tel: 01780 756777
www.cips.org

Chartered Management Institute
Management House
Cottingham Road
Corby NN17 1TT
Tel: 01536 204222
www.managers.org.uk

Chartered Quality Institute
2nd Floor North
Chancery Exchange
10 Furnival Street
London EC4A 1AB
Tel: 020 7245 6722
www.thecqi.org

Confederation of British Industry
Cannon Place
78 Cannon Street
London EC4N 6HN
Tel: 020 7379 7400
www.cbi.org.uk

Department for the Economy
Netherleigh
Massey Avenue
Belfast BT4 2JP
Tel: 028 9052 9900
www.economy-ni.gov.uk

Department for Communities
Lighthouse Building
1 Cromac Place
Gasworks Business Park
Ormeau Road
Belfast BT7 2JB
Tel: 028 9082 9000
www.communities-ni.gov.uk

Federation of Small Businesses
Sir Frank Whittle Way
Blackpool FY4 2FE
Tel: 0808 20 20 888
www.fsb.org.uk

Freight Transport Association
Hermes House
St John's Road
Tunbridge Wells TN4 9UZ
Tel: 03717 112222
www.fta.co.uk

Higher Education Funding Council for Wales
Tŷ Aron
Bedwas Road
Bedwas
Caerphilly CF83 8WT
Tel: 029 2085 9696
www.hefcw.ac.uk

Institute of Administrative Management
Coppice House
Halesfield 7
Telford TF7 4NA
Tel: 01952 797396
www.instam.org

Institute of Chartered Secretaries and Administrators
Saffron House
6–10 Kirby Street
London EC1N 8TS
Tel: 020 7580 4741
www.icsa.org.uk

Institute of Credit Management
The Water Mill
Station Road
South Luffenham LE15 8NB
Tel: 01780 722900
www.icm.org.uk

Institute of Directors
116 Pall Mall
London SW1Y 5ED
Tel: 020 7766 8866
www.iod.com

Institute of Management Services
Brooke House
24 Dam Street
Lichfield WS13 6AA
Tel: 01543 266909
www.ims-productivity.com

Institute of Materials, Minerals and Mining
1 Carlton House Terrace
London SW1Y 5DB
Tel: 020 7451 7300
www.iom3.org

Management Consultancies Association
5th Floor
36–38 Cornhill
London EC3V 3NG
Tel: 020 7645 7950
www.mca.org.uk

Office for Students
External Relations Department
Nicholson House
Lime Kiln Close
Stoke Gifford
Bristol BS34 8SR
Tel: 0117 931 7317
www.hefce.ac.uk

Operational Research Society
Seymour House
12 Edward Street
Birmingham B1 2RX
Tel: 0121 233 9300
www.theorsociety.com

Prince's Trust
18 Park Square East
London NW1 4LH
Tel: 020 7543 1234
www.princes-trust.org.uk

Scottish Funding Council
Donaldson House
97 Haymarket Terrace
Edinburgh EH12 5HD
Tel: 0131 313 6500
www.sfc.ac.uk

Work Foundation
21 Palmer Street
London SW1H 0AD
Tel: 0203 907 0710
www.theworkfoundation.com

Glossary

Adjustment
A UCAS process allowing students who met and exceeded conditions of their firm choice to be considered by alternative courses, without having to let go of their firm choice.

Administration
A process which allows struggling companies to attempt a comeback by allowing them to continue to operate under close supervision. Companies in administration need permission from a court before they can be dissolved.

Apply
UCAS' online applications system, which students use to apply to their university choices by the appropriate closing date (see the UCAS website for more details). You can apply for up to five choices for all courses, except medicine, dentistry and veterinary science/medicine (which are limited to a maximum of four choices, although you can make another subject your fifth choice).

Clearing
A UCAS system that allows students who are not holding any offers to try to get a place on a course with remaining vacancies.

Confederation of British Industry (CBI)
A lobbying organisation that looks after the interests of British businesses at home and overseas. By working with government bodies and legislators it seeks to promote conditions in which British business can compete and thrive.

Extra
A UCAS process that allows you to add one extra choice at a time (between February and June) if you are holding no offers.

IMF
The International Monetary Fund. An organisation set up after World War II to provide financial assistance to governments. The IMF has provided rescue loans to developing countries with debt issues, and more recently has been involved in bailouts for EU governments during the European debt crisis.

Macroeconomics
The study of economic issues across a whole economy. It looks at economy-wide patterns in areas such as trade.

Microeconomics

The study of choices made by individuals and businesses in order to better understand behaviour. Microeconomists often use this sort of information to understand supply and demand in particular markets (e.g. oil or coffee) and to make predictions about how markets will react to external influences.

Personal statement

This is where you have 47 lines (or 4,000 characters including spaces, whichever you use first) to convince the five universities you are applying to that you are right for the course.

Recession

A slowdown in economic activity. A country is technically in recession following two consecutive periods of negative growth.

Track

UCAS service that enables you to track the progress of your application once it has been submitted. Any interview invitations or offers you receive will be posted here. You will then need to use Track to reply to all offers. On results day, you will receive a notification from Track confirming whether you have a place on your firm or insurance choice.

UCAS

Universities and Colleges Admissions Service.

Notes